THE SIGNIFICANCE OF SENSE
Meaning, Modality, and Morality

CONTEMPORARY PHILOSOPHY

General Editor
Max Black, Cornell University

THE SIGNIFICANCE OF SENSE

Meaning, Modality, and Morality

By Roger Wertheimer

Cornell University Press

ITHACA AND LONDON

First published 1972 by Cornell University Press.
Published in the United Kingdom by Cornell University Press Ltd.,
2–4 Brook Street, London W1Y 1AA.

International Standard Book Number 0-8014-0672-2
Library of Congress Catalog Card Number 70-162541

PRINTED IN THE UNITED STATES OF AMERICA
BY VAIL-BALLOU PRESS, INC.

To Stashu and
Christabobble

Acknowledgments

THIS book is a more polished and more polite version of a manuscript which various people have influenced in various ways. Stanley Cavell and Rogers Albritton advised me on the earliest drafts. From Rogers especially, as a teacher and even more as a friend, I have benefited far beyond the scope of this book or anything else I might write.

I must also thank those other teachers whose instruction has had a substantial, though indirect, effect on this book: most particularly David Sachs, Roderick Firth, Hilary Putnam, and John Rawls.

I am grateful as well to Noam Chomsky and Haj Ross, who freely gave of their time to explain to me that what I didn't know about syntax (which was and is considerable) I didn't need to know, and, anyway, no one else knew either.

My thanks also to Marshall Cohen, William Alston, Hector-Neri Casteñeda, Gil Harmon, and Max Black for their com-

Acknowledgments

ments and points of view which have guided my later revisions. I am especially appreciative of John Cooper's careful and thorough criticisms, which were as sensitive as they were sensible.

Finally, to my wife, who aided and abetted me through so many periods of perversity—thank you, dear woman.

ROGER WERTHEIMER

Portland, Oregon

Contents

Introduction

The key words in morals are 'good', 'right', and 'ought'.
—J. D. Mabbott, *An Introduction to Ethics*

THE moral of the story I shall tell is that the story would be without philosophical interest were it not that many philosophers have thought otherwise. That moral is of philosophical interest, but once it is drawn, the story ceases to be of interest. Still, the tale must be told in order to draw its moral.

This is not an expression of modesty or contempt. At most it betrays a preference for a certain use of the word 'philosophical', a preference needing no defense because the issue is not whether the questions I ask and the answers I give are philosophical. The questions I ask are in center stage of Anglo-American academic moral philosophy in this century; they are questions about language and meaning and the justification of moral judgments. Nor is the issue whether the answers I give are interesting and important. Such is the life of the mind that the answer to a question will almost inevitably seem interesting and important to a man who, whatever his impetus may have been, is now preoccupied with the question—more so if

Introduction

he has devoted the better part of his intellectual career to answering it and defending his answer to it. Rather, the issue is whether the questions have the kind of answers that led certain philosophers—call them meta-ethicists—to ask the questions in the first place. The issue in its most general form is whether some rules of language have some bearing on the nature of morality.

Understandably, meta-ethicists are as one in their belief in the existence of such rules. And since the words 'good', 'right', and 'ought' figure prominently in talk about moral matters, meta-ethicists agree that some of these rules concern the meanings of these words. But they disagree about what the rules are, partly because they espouse opposing semantic theories. Some say that semantic rules connect those words to the names of certain empirical (i.e., ostensibly nonethical) properties, thereby guaranteeing the inference of certain moral judgments from certain factual judgments. Others say that, on the contrary, the rules prohibit any such inference, and to violate these rules is to commit the naturalistic fallacy. (See Chapter One.)

The questions I shall ask are meta-ethical ones. And, as is inevitable, my answers are based on linguistic theories that are certainly incomplete and probably incorrect, at least in parts. (However, they are, I think, the best available hypotheses on the workings of language.) With these theories I shall construct a rule concerning the word 'ought' and some related words. A violation of this rule can properly be said to constitute a commission of the naturalistic fallacy. Yet, in one respect, what I shall be doing is unlike meta-ethics, for the rule I shall propound reveals absolutely nothing about the nature of morality. The questions do not elicit answers that make the questions worth the asking. And since I think that no legitimate seman-

tic rule reveals something about the nature of morality, I see
no point in doing meta-ethics. However, I do not pretend to
prove this general claim; I restrict my remarks to 'ought' and a
few other words.

The heart of my argument, Chapter Three, is devoted to
establishing a single empirical truth: the modal auxiliary verb
'ought' is univocal in contemporary standard English; it means
the same in 'You ought not to harm others.' as it does in 'The
roast ought to be done by now.', 'This proposition ought to be
derivable from those premises.', and every other sentence in
which it appears. Given this, I show in Chapter Four that the
semantic principles governing derivations of 'ought' propositions reveal nothing about the nature of morality—or rather,
whatever they show about morality they show about geology,
geometry, gastronomy, and every other subject. In other words,
either the principles disclose nothing distinctive about morality
(in which case meta-ethics is unproductive) or the principles
are not semantic ones (in which case meta-ethics is irrelevant.)

As something of an epilogue, in the last chapter I duplicate
this argument with the word 'right' (the adjectival modifier
whose antonym is 'wrong') by showing that it is univocal, that
it means the same in 'What he said is right.' as it does in 'What
he did is right.'. I would not have spent myself on a second unproductive labor were I not motivated by a principle: If enough
is good, more is better. By inventorying two-thirds of the supposedly central moral vocabulary,* I hoped my readers might

* The third word is 'good'. I ignore it since sufficient work has been
done on it by others. Though no single account has received general
acceptance, the differences between the more plausible accounts do not
seem significant for ethics. By now it seems clear enough that nothing
about the meaning of this word makes naturalism untenable. I suggest
that agreement on the correct account must await production of and
agreement on a fairly strong semantic theory. I, for one, would be un-

more willingly make the appropriate induction, forsake their
O.E.D.'s, and bethink themselves about matters that matter.
Yet, I confess that in this case my ambitions exceed my abilities:
my account of 'right' is as speculative as it is plausible, because
my conclusions are in line with, but outstrip, what is well
established in syntactical theory. But, were it not for that gap, I
would say that the evidence for the univocity of 'right' is
stronger than that for 'ought'.

Before embarking on my argument, I think it necessary to
make the cheap concession that, even if my accounts of 'ought'
and 'right' are correct, it does not follow that these words are
univocal. It does not follow because, as should be obvious and
will become more so, our present homemade notions of univocity, ambiguity, meaning, sense, and the like are not yet
finely enough honed to permit decisive adjudication of such
cases. Our pretheoretical vocabulary for describing our vocabulary is a crude instrument, and it may well be that an
adequate semantic theory would have us segregate into separate
senses what I call the same sense. For that matter, it may well
be that an adequate semantic theory would divest itself of such
notions altogether in favor of some more manageable model
of language. Such possibilities can be ignored with impunity
here (though not everywhere), since, even if realized, the philosophical implications of my argument would not be materially
affected. My strategy is, in effect, to give a partial implicit
definition of univocity in Chapter Two, and then show that
'ought' and 'right' meet these intuitively acceptable requirements. In short, I call them univocal because, for all my intents

------

satisfied with any account which failed to distinguish 'good' from a score
of other words like 'nice' and 'fine'. Partly because I can't distinguish
'right' from 'correct', I consider my work on 'right' incomplete.

and purposes, they behave as they would if they were univocal. So, a reader with other intents and purposes not incompatible with mine might refuse to call them univocal without my begrudging him his balk.

One

The Philosophical Context

> It's rather a pity that people are apt to invoke a new use of language whenever they feel so inclined, to help them out of this, that, or the other well-known philosophical tangle.
>
> J. L. Austin, "Performative Utterances"

PRIOR to this century a great deal had been written about what things are morally right and ought to be done: much of it profound, and some of it true, but little of it bearing on the meanings of 'right' and 'ought'. Not that one can't catch an earlier philosopher slipping into the formal mode when announcing his theory about morality. Rather, it is only since Sidgwick and Moore that moral philosophers have delivered their semantic doctrines with much insistence; those of their predecessors are infrequent and incidental. A utilitarian may have said that 'right' means 'conformable to the principle of utility'; a subjectivist that it means 'approved of by myself'; a relativist that it means 'approved of by my society'; and so on. Such formulas compete for our acceptance only if we assume (since it goes unargued) that the same uses of 'right' are intended by each theorist, and that 'right' is univocal over them all. More importantly, the theories, *sans* semantic formulas, need not be rivals; they may be about separable aspects of morality. The utilitarian may be propounding a fundamental criterion of morally right actions, while the subjectivist pictures moral judgments and principles as an expression of an individual's attitudes, and the relativist focuses on the role of a culture in the formation of an individual's attitudes and beliefs. When a writer like Bentham, albeit he expresses linguistic concerns elsewhere, declares that "the words *ought* and *right* . . . have a meaning" only when interpreted as applying solely to actions conformable to the principle of utility,[1] I read him as I would a political scientist who declares that the word *police* has a meaning only when interpreted as applying solely to organizations within an advanced industrialized nation. Even Hume, despite his many (often incompatible) linguistic claims about our moral vocabulary, is manifestly more a psychologist than a semanticist. Such writers may occasionally encapsulate their moral theories in semantic equations, but the intuitions and arguments on which their theories rest are not linguistic ones.

Sidgwick and Moore properly reproved their precursors for their infelicitous diction and, in so doing, made their successors self-conscious of their speech. But in their move toward greater precision, philosophers carried what had been a peripheral infirmity to the center of debate. Again, the evidence does not suggest that earlier moral philosophers thought through the consequences of their linguistic claims, much less that they seriously intended to validate their moral judgments via some lexicographical legerdemain. Yet, once Moore and succeeding intuitionists labeled as naturalistic and criticized any theory that defined an ostensibly ethical term by reference to an ostensibly non-ethical property, naturalists seemed to be everywhere that intuitionists and their noncognitivist allies were not. That so many stood ready to man a meta-ethical position might seem an instance of discovering and defending what one had meant all along, and thus a counterindication to the history I have sketched. But what we are and mean are plastic; they alter in unrecorded ways with the pressures of an argument. And, in this instance, the argument has seemed formidable in a time and place in which metaphysical distinctions (such as that between fact and value) were being translated en bloc into logico-semantic ones.

I do not deny, indeed I insist, that the various meta-ethical theories have readily traceable roots in nonlinguistic moral theories. They are theories of morality expressed in and defended by semantic formulas, but the intuitions which foster them and the intentions which direct them are unconnected with matters of meaning. And, since why we ask a question will bias where and how we look for its answer, even the meta-ethicists' methods have been slanted by their philosophical motivations. It is of some importance, then, that every philosophical discussion of 'ought' and 'right' is set in an ethical context. Not surprisingly, the evidence and arguments adduced in support and refutation of the semantic formulas have been more philosophical and moral than linguistic in character. This has become somewhat less true as meta-ethicists have gradually replaced a mix of metaphysical, ethical, and epistemological considerations with more systematic studies of syntax, sentence-environments, and speech contexts. (Cf. discussions of 'good' ca. 1905 and ca. 1965.) Still, certain habits persist. Although meta-ethicists chronically make mention of 'right' and 'ought', generally they subject only 'good' to a sustained, intensive ex-

3

amination, as though once they had 'good' well in hand, an understanding of 'right' and 'ought' would follow as a matter of course.*

All this tends to cast doubt on the status of the meta-ethicists' proposals as *semantic* theses.† I shall not develop that suggestion. I take them to be full-blooded, deliberate, albeit erroneous, semantic theses guided by philosophical interests. So, I reserve the labels 'intuitionist' and 'noncognitivist' for specifically meta-ethical theories, whatever their non-linguistic lineage. But, since naturalism has served as the foil of intuitionism and noncognitivism, I shall call someone a naturalist if he disavows intuitionism and noncognitivism, whatever other, if any, meta-ethical teachings he accepts. Put more positively and more narrowly, if somewhat crudely, a theory is naturalistic if it claims that many (if not all) moral judgments have a genuine truth-value knowable by rational procedures involving reference primarily to the empirical facts of human situations. To be sure, intuitionists and noncognitivists suppose that a plausible naturalistic theory must be naturalistic

---

* It is equally worthy of note that epistemologists concentrate on the word 'true', though it is far from obvious why true statements should be more deserving of philosophical attention than right (or correct) answers, descriptions, explanations, and so on.

† Among contemporary meta-ethicists, some claim a concern with moral concepts, e.g., the concepts of ought and right, while denying any concern for the semantics of words, e.g., 'ought' and 'right'. I would forsake imperialistic ambitions and grudgingly grant the irrelevance of my work to theirs if their claim were intelligible to me. But, theoretical considerations aside, I frankly do not understand what is meant by 'the concept of ought' and 'the concept of right' unless they be neologisms for 'the meaning of 'ought' ' and 'the meaning of 'right' '. Matters would be otherwise were I discussing, for example, 'obligation' and 'right' (as in 'a civil right'), for I recognize concepts associated with and distinguishable from the meanings of these words.

in Moore's sense (i.e., it must define an ostensibly ethical term by reference to an ostensibly non-ethical property). And many a naturalist has allowed his opponents to dictate the rules of battle—and, thus, the terms of surrender. But to show that naturalism must be Moorian naturalism, it must be shown that meta-ethical (i.e., semantic) issues are relevant to the task of naturalism. This I wish to deny.

I shall now begin inspecting first intuitionism and then non-cognitivism, while explaining naturalism only in its role as their foil. The rationale for this format is that only intuitionism and noncognitivism are committed to ambiguist * accounts of 'right' and 'ought'. My coverage of these theories could be faulted on various counts. The theories are viewed only in the light of their ambiguist views on 'right' and 'ought'—an eccentric perspective. Their propounders did not view them this way; disputes within each theory lie hidden from view. Had I larger ambitions, a more well-balanced, scholarly history would be in order, but my intention is little more than that of documenting the relevance of subsequent chapters to the concerns of other philosophers. So, though the perspective is eccentric and unflattering, it is not unjust if the truth, or at least the defensibility or plausibility of the theories is linked to their doctrines on 'right' and 'ought'. I explore the doctrines largely by criticizing them; the criticism is a mode of exploration, not refutation. If I have a refutation of these doctrines or the larger theories, it is located in later chapters.†

---

* I call a person or theory that claims an expression w has one (more than one) sense *univocalist* (*ambiguist*) regarding w.

† Kuhn's point that scientific theories are replaced, not refuted, applies, I think, to philosophical theories as well. The difference is a relative one—the degree to which a theory goes out of fashion.

The Significance of Sense

Intuitionism is best understood as an outcropping of referential theories of meaning according to which the fundamental linguistic relation is that between a name and an object, an ultimate particular. In line with this, intuitionism conceives morality in terms of a set of ultimate, *sui generis* properties (or relations), the names of which are the supposedly central items of the moral lexicon: 'good', 'right', and 'ought'. Each of these words either names a simple, discrete, non-natural property or is definable solely by reference to one of the other of them which is such a name. Thus, none of them can be defined using only words naming properties not named by these words. And thus, no moral judgment is derivable from a set of nonmoral judgments (i.e., judgments containing no word naming an ethical property or definable in terms of such a name). So, no moral judgment is derivable from factual judgments alone. To apprehend the truth of a moral judgment one must, at some point, perform a special act of cognition, an intuition, by which one discerns the presence or absence of a non-natural moral property.

Whatever appeal this theory may have as an analysis of moral judgments, it is obviously without any as an analysis of nonmoral judgments in which 'right' and 'ought' appear. Plainly, no act of intuition is required for the realization that punting is the right thing to do (one ought to punt) on a fourth-and-forty situation in the first quarter, or that a knife is not the right utensil (one ought not to use a knife) for eating peas at high table. Plainly, intuitionists take themselves to be talking about words which name properties (or relations) common to only moral things.

Thus, intuitionism is wedded to what I call the Doctrine of Moral Senses (hereafter, DMS). The DMS is the thesis that 'right' and 'ought' (and perhaps other words) are ambiguous;

6

each of them has (at least) two senses: a moral sense and a nonmoral sense. The moral sense is the one meant when the word is used morally. A rough criterion for distinguishing the moral from the nonmoral *uses* of a word is this: A word is being used morally if and only if either the words 'moral' or 'morally' appear in the utterance as modifiers of the word or could be so inserted without altering what the speaker means. Compare: 'When I say that it is wrong for us to be fighting in Vietnam, I mean it is morally wrong.'. Call this the M-criterion.

The DMS is explicitly stated in the writings of many intuitionists, sometimes carefully (e.g., Prichard [2]), sometimes not.* But even if not presented, its presence is detectable, since intuitionists defend other doctrines whose plausibility presupposes its acceptance. A case in point is the peculiar idea, commonly held by intuitionists, that 'right' and 'ought' are something like adjectival and verbal forms of 'duty' and 'obligation', just as 'before' is the prepositional counterpart of 'precede'.[4] And, more to the point, as noted, the central doctrines of intuitionism are tied to the DMS. The converse does not hold; although only intuitionism requires the DMS, some naturalists and noncognitivists have accepted versions of it.

A couple of observations on the M-criterion: First, it divides the uses, the appearances of a word (i.e., the class of the word-tokens) into two sets. It can also divide whole utterances, judgments, and other linguistic entities into two sets. However, it does not in any way imply a division of the meaning or sense of the members of the sets. We use the words 'moral' and 'morally' as ways of indicating what *we*, the speaker, mean

---

* E. G. Ross says he is concerned only with the sense 'right' has when "applied to acts," [3] but being applied to acts is neither necessary (since it is applicable to institutions, policies, and so forth) nor sufficient (since acts can be nonmorally right) for what, evidently, he has in mind.

by our utterances, by the words we utter. They signal the kinds of considerations we take as relevant in support or confutation of our utterances. And conversely, what *we mean* by our utterances is evidenced by the kinds of considerations we accept as relevant. Intuitionists, however, have appealed to such evidence to argue that the *words* modified by 'moral' and 'morally' *have two meanings*. Indeed, every argument made for the DMS would have us conflate what a speaker means by the words he utters with what the words he utters mean. That merger seems ill advised.

If what we mean were always what our words mean, then irony and much, much more would be impossible. If I say, 'We'll have a bash.', and you ask 'What do you mean 'we'?', and I reply, 'I mean all the girls in Hadassah except for Celeste and Rosalie and maybe one or two others.', my reply gives what I mean, not what the word 'we' means. The English pronoun 'we' is not ambiguous. Further, once having accepted such evidence as proof of an ambiguity, fertile minds will fetch up senses without end. Ewing counts ten senses of 'good' and three senses of 'right' and 'ought' in their moral uses alone; [5] his colleagues have added still others.

An intuitionist is particularly prone to this confusion since he generally supposes that the meaning of a word is a mental entity (an idea or concept) which fixes the relation between a word and the object it names. Thus, his method of ascertaining the meaning is simply to introspect what he means when he uses the word.* And his standard procedure for testing any proposed definition is to rivet his attention onto the meanings of the definiens and the definiendum and ask

---

* See Ewing: "All I can say is that when I try to see what I mean when I use ethical terms I find that I have present to my consciousness an idea generically different from any empirical psychological concepts." [6]

whether the objects before his mind number more than one.*

One other point about the M-criterion: As would any alternative linguistic criterion, it disguises and distorts a difference it is meant to capture. The distinction between the moral and the nonmoral is neither simple nor clear nor sharp; it is sometimes a matter of degree, sometimes of kind. Cases form a continuum; better: continua, for the difference is multidimensional, since the moral contrasts not only with the prudential, but also with the aesthetic, the epistemological, the legal, the conventional, etc., and each contrast has its own character. As used by philosophers, 'moral' and 'morally' are terms of art. In lay speech these words are vague and ambiguous and are understood differently by different people. And for any one person their use may be governed by subtle and elusive considerations. For example, I am willing to say that gross inequities in the tax structure (e.g., the oil depletion allowance) are a moral matter, and that Congress ought to undo them, but I do not believe that Congress morally ought to undo them. Also, I am willing to *believe* that it's morally wrong to heist a Hershey bar, and would *say* that it's wrong to heist a Hershey bar, but, except perhaps in a philosophical discussion, I would not *say* that it's morally wrong to do it. (I do not wish to make a moral issue out of what is a moral issue.) So, would we, in order to satisfy what motivates the DMS, need to have not merely two senses of 'right' and 'ought', but a string of senses? Or put it this way: suppose that

---

* Applied to my definition of 'ought' (Chapter Three) the question seems more moot than open. My definiens is so damnably involved that when I—even I who conceived it (bit by bit)—hold it up for inspection before my mind's eye, my synapses snap and fizzle and the image flickers and blurs, whereas when I bethink myself of the meaning of 'ought' directly, I draw a blank. But then, if, in the last analysis, a blank and a blur leave little to choose between, my account might yet pass muster.

instead of 'right' and 'ought', for clarity's sake we had four words, 'mright', 'mought', 'nright', 'nought', whose uses were identical, respectively, to the moral uses of 'right' and 'ought' and the nonmoral uses of 'right' and 'ought'. Could we still say and express what we are now able to say and express? *

These points are sharpened by seeing how the intuitionists characterize the two senses. So far we have only the bare claim that certain words have a moral sense in their moral uses and a nonmoral sense in their nonmoral uses. That claim is incomplete and gratuitous unless accompanied by some characterization of the two senses. The characterizations need not be definitions; one might hold the words to be undefinable (whatever that might mean) in one or more of their senses. But some difference must be described if the purported distinction is not to be idle.

The senses must be of a quite specific sort to satisfy the demands of intuitionism, for it holds that a logico-semantic principle prohibits derivations of moral judgments from factual judgments. The intuitionist paradigms of a moral judgment are utterances of the form, 'N ought to X' and 'X is the right thing for N to do'. But, apparently, some utterances of that form (e.g., nonmoral judgments) are derivable from factual judgments (e.g., judgments about the agent's ends conjoined with judgments about the means for securing those ends). But if judgments of that form are unequivocal and *some* are derivable from factual judgments, then no logico-semantic principle could void derivations of other (e.g., moral) judgments of that form from factual judgments. Intuitionism requires a DMS that avoids this consequence.

---

* The questions must do duty for an argument, since the required argument would consist of a raft of elaborate and subtle examples. The point at issue is important but not sufficiently central to warrant the space.

The Philosophical Context

The nonmoral sense seems easily taken care of because it can plausibly be supposed that the truth-conditions of a nonmoral judgment about what an agent ought to do (what it is right for him to do) consist solely of the agent's ends (desires, wants, purposes, interests) and the means for securing those ends. So, intuitionists identify the meaning of the nonmoral judgment with the meaning of a statement expressing that means-ends relation. Thus, Prichard says that the nonmoral judgment 'I ought to do so and so.' means the same as 'If I do not do so and so, my purposes will not be realized.'.[7] Intuitionists cannot say that the truth of the latter serves as merely a reason supporting the truth of the former, for that would leave open the logical problem of *how* it can serve as a reason (i.e., how the 'ought' is derived from the 'is')—and that is a problem they want to bury. On this issue, as far as I can ascertain, every advocate of the DMS sides with the intuitionists.*

It would be unfair to accord this claim more attention than its propounders have. A few quick cases should suffice to cast doubt on this characterization of the nonmoral sense, for not every such nonmoral judgment depends for its truth on the agent's ends. Some such judgments can be legitimately maintained even when the speaker acknowledges that N's doing X does not accord with N's ends.

A: I ought to punch you in the nose for that stunt, but I won't only because your sister would never forgive me. (N.B.: A won't because it is contrary to his

---

* Note that this definition flunks the intuitionists' favorite test for an adequate definition. I can grant that if I do not do so and so, my purposes will not be realized, and still meaningfully ask whether I ought to do it. The intuitionist may insist that my question employs the moral sense of 'ought', but how is he to show that in a non–question-begging way?

interests, but A does not deny that he ought to for that reason, for A does not deny it at all.)

B: You ought to shave.

C: Ahh, I hate to shave.

B: But you look like hell.

C: So what? I don't give a damn how I look.

B: You're impossible. Just look at yourself in the mirror.

C: O.K., so I'm looking. So I've got a day's growth. So?

B: So shave.

D: You ought to believe what he told you.

E: Why should I?

D: Because he's right, that's why.

E: Yeah, well I don't want to believe it.

D: What the hell do you mean by that!

E: Listen, if he's right, then I've been wrong all along and I've made a damn fool of myself, and I couldn't go on if I thought that.

D: Hmm . . . well . . . I'm sorry, but I don't know what you can do about it.

F: What's wrong with you! That's not the right tempo. You ought to be playing it andante.

G: But I rather like it this way.

F: NO! NO! NO! Listen to what you are doing! It's all wrong! Can't you hear that?

G: But you don't understand. It really makes me feel all warm and bubbly inside to play it this way.

F: What is this nonsense?! Have you gone mad?! Here I am trying to produce a decent piece of music and my conductor has gone bananas. Now quit clowning around and play the piece right. If you don't want to

play it the way you ought to play it, then I'll get someone else.

It is only on the moral sense that advocates of the DMS
diverge. Again, the intuitionist moral sense must be such that
moral judgments have a truth-value not determinable via
factual judgments. So intuitionists insist that in their moral
uses 'right' and 'ought' refer to or are definable solely by
reference to non-natural properties or relations, i.e., properties
or relations having no logico-semantic relation to natural properties or relations. A quite caliginous characterization, since
intuitionists have never satisfactorily elucidated their term
'natural'.

Some purchase on the intuitionist thesis is provided by
understanding what it opposes: naturalist versions of the DMS.
Like intuitionists, many naturalists accept the DMS. Moorian
naturalism is committed to it. The definitions offered by these
naturalists (e.g., 'right' means 'productive of the greatest hap-
piness') have comic consequences when applied to nonmoral
cases such as, 'Would you kindly instruct me in the right way
to torture a prisoner.'. And, as I said, these naturalists accept
the intuitionists' characterization of the nonmoral sense.
Further, these naturalists operate with essentially the same
semantic theory as the intuitionists: 'right' and 'ought' are
treated as names of properties or relations (which leaves these
naturalists fairly defenseless against the intuitionists). And,
like the intuitionists, these naturalists look at the reasons we
accept in support of our moral judgments, and confuse what
a speaker means by the words he utters with what the words
he utters mean.

At this juncture the various naturalist theories part company
from each other and from intuitionism. Each theory focuses

on a different feature of morality, and records its observations (some of which may be faulty) in a semantic formula. So, granting this description of the dispute, the question then is, What aspect of morality does intuitionism focus upon? What is the feature whose lack is common and confined to naturalistic versions of the DMS and accounts for their rejection by intuitionists?

My answer may not gain currency, since, as intuitionists are traditionally read, a standard objection to their DMS is that it permits no explanation of why something's being morally right or being something one morally ought to do constitutes a reason for action. Noncognitivists in particular have insisted that a moral judgment which merely records the possession of a property, non-natural or otherwise, by an object would not provide a reason for acting except in special circumstances, and thus would not be a moral judgment. But all this seems wrongheaded to me, for I take it that a non-natural property is supposed to be one the possession of which could not but be a reason for action.* Precisely because intuitionists regarded natural properties as being devoid of that feature, they regarded them as unfit to define ethical terms.

My suggestion is that the intuitionists' DMS is meant to be a semantic counterpart of Kant's distinction between categorical and hypothetical imperatives. Prichard (mistakenly, I think) presents the DMS as simply Kantian exegesis;[10] his characterization of the nonmoral sense clearly captures the force of a

---

* Cf. Sidgwick: "When I speak of the cognition or judgment that 'X ought to be done'—in the stricter ethical sense of the term ought—as a 'dictate' or 'precept' of reason to the persons to whom it relates, I imply that in rational beings as such this cognition gives an impulse or motive to action."[8] And Ewing: " "Good" in its non-natural sense or senses carries with it the notion that the good thing *ought* not to be wantonly sacrificed, but, other things being equal, pursued."[9]

hypothetical imperative. And intuitionists generally seem possessed of a quite Kantian concern for the categorical nature of moral judgments. (Whatever their disagreements with Kant, intuitionists as a group seem the most Kantian of meta-ethicists in tone and outlook.) So the meaning of the moral terms must be such as to vouchsafe the categorical character of the judgments in which they appear. The trouble with any naturalistic DMS, in the eyes of intuitionists, is its inevitable vindication of heteronymous substantive moral principles, for the semantic identification of a moral property with an ostensibly nonmoral property must be transformable into a nonmoral reason for acting in conformity with a moral judgment. That naturalistic doctrines would justify moral principles by linguistic fiat is objectionable because the linguistic legislation lacks the requisite categorical status.* More objectionable still, the moral principles so generated cannot impose absolute, unconditional requirements, because no natural property is such that its possession provides a reason for acting for any rational being independently of his ends.† Naturalistic ethical principles lack the special quality of ethical principles.‡

---

* Cf. Moore: "In so far as (naturalists) tell us how we ought to act, their teaching is truly ethical. . . . But how perfectly absurd is the reason they give for it! 'You are to do this, because most people use a certain word to denote conduct such as this.' " [11]

† Cf. Ewing: "What is missing from any naturalist or subjectivist account? . . . At any rate the most important (element) is the concept of obligation," and following remarks.[12]

‡ Cf. Moore: "[Naturalism] is inconsistent with the possibility of any Ethics whatsoever." [13] Yet Moore does not neatly fit the above description for the very reason that Ross rightly reproved him: Moore's thorough-going consequentialism is inconsistent with a thorough-going intuitionism. His definition of 'right' as 'cause of a good result' is at odds with his standards for definitions and reduces substantive moral principles to a species of hypothetical imperative.

The Significance of Sense

I shall not rebut this characterization here. From the vantage point of contemporary linguistics it beggars the imagination to conceive of the intuitionists' DMS as a candidate for a semantic account of 'right' or 'ought'. (That sounds like a harsh judgment; I mean it to be an unprejudicial statement of fact.) Indeed, were it not for the use to which intuitionists put their DMS, I would be dissuaded from treating it as a semantic account altogether. After all, they offered no evidence or arguments for it save one, a presumed refutation of naturalism—unless an invitation to introspection is an argument. (Unhappily, the introspection yields, at very best, inconclusive results. There are those among us who report no intuition of non-natural properties. And even among those with the requisite clarity of mind and purity of heart, it would remain a live possibility that with the same ethical term different non-natural properties were being referred to by different persons or by the same person at different times—which casts doubt on whether such properties could play a role in our use of language.) In any case, the bulk of intuitionistic writing is critical, not constructive. The truth of their DMS and the existence of non-natural properties are supposed to follow from the falsity of naturalism. But their refutation of naturalism rests on an invalid test of definitions and an unwarranted induction as to the consequences of any naturalistic definition. The proper response to intuitionism is to present adequate naturalistic definitions. I shall make that response in a later chapter.

Noncognitivism has to be approached somewhat differently if only because it developed later than intuitionism and profited from its mistakes and from the teachings of more recent and more sophisticated linguistic theories. In consequence, the semantic theses of noncognitivism are generally more sophisticated and more attentive to the details of linguistic usage. There are exceptions: some noncognitivist theses are simply straightforward deductions from defective linguistic theories. Ayer's emotivism, for example, is presented as just another consequence of the verificationist theory of meaning; the particular features of 'right' and 'ought' receive little attention beyond the observation that moral judgments in which they appear are not subject to empirical tests.[14]

Moreover, as the foregoing suggests, 'noncognitivism' is a rubric encompassing a more motley clump of theories. As with intuitionism, each linguistic theory spawns a set of similar but slightly divergent meta-ethical theses. But unlike intuitionism, noncognitivist theses may be fathered by a variety of linguistic theories. Thus the internecine quarrels within noncognitivism are more severe than those within intuitionism, and, hence, my survey here must be more selective. For instance, many of the earlier noncognitivist theses seem committed to a version of the DMS, since they hold that utterances in which 'right' and 'ought' appear are meaningless, a contention without credibility if it covers nonmoral cases like, 'If you like being depressed, then you ought to ride the New York subways.'. The more recent vintages of noncognitivism have forsaken the DMS, sometimes explicitly,* sometimes not. Often their position on the matter is obscured by their tendency to speak of different *uses* rather than *senses* of a word, and by their silence on the relation between a use of a word and a sense of the word. But since they *can* abandon the DMS, I won't accuse them of adopting it. However, their position obliges them to split the uses of 'right' and 'ought' at another point. Since these recent theories are generally regarded, at least at present,

---

* See Hare's critique of Prichard.[15]

as the most plausible versions of noncognitivism, my remarks will be confined to them.

Latter-day noncognitivists have identified themselves with the writings of Austin and the later Wittgenstein. Out of Wittgenstein's "thesis" that the meaning of a word is its use and Austin's theory of speech acts they have molded a meta-ethical theory about the meanings of the supposedly central words of moral discourse. According to the noncognitivists, the function of utterances containing words like 'right' and 'ought' is to guide conduct: to prescribe, evaluate, advise, condemn, commend, etc.* Since they have this special use not just in moral contexts but in practical contexts in general, they can be univocal over all their practical uses.† Further, since their special meaning is evidenced by their special connection with certain illocutions,‡ words which lack that special

---

* I shall not worry overmuch about these alternative functions, though these writers do. Hare holds that each of the trio 'good', 'right', and 'ought' has a prescriptive function. Mayo holds that only 'right' and 'ought' have a prescriptive function, whereas 'good' has an evaluative function. Taylor holds that only 'ought' has a prescriptive function, whereas 'right' and 'good' have an evaluative function. Nowell-Smith holds that all these positions are too rigid. I hold that the issue is unmanageable if one presupposes, as many writers apparently do, that these functions are mutually exclusive, that the same utterance cannot be both an evaluation and a prescription—and a statement.

† However, they need not be univocal for that reason. Just as some intuitionists list multiple moral senses of 'right' and 'ought', some noncognitivists delineate senses within the practical uses of these words. Such subsidiary lines of demarcation may but need not coincide with that set by the M-criterion.

‡ The term 'illocution' refers to a linguistic entity (e.g., a statement, a condemnation) which is the product of a correlative speech act (e.g., stating, condemning) which consists of the utterance of certain words in certain circumstances. In uttering the words one performs the speech act and produces the illocution. The term 'illocution' derives from J. L. Austin's *How to Do Things with Words*.

connection must have a quite different kind of meaning.

Practical discourse is of a logically different kind from that of nonpractical discourse. Practical discourse is concerned with decision and action, with changing or preserving the world. The grammatical paradigm here is the imperative mood. And value judgments (i.e., utterances containing words like 'right' and 'ought') are a species of practical discourse. Contrasted with this, nonpractical discourse serves to describe the world. This is the domain of factual judgments, of statements, assertions, and descriptions possessing a genuine truth-value in virtue of their correspondence (or lack of it) with the facts of the world in which we choose and act. The grammatical paradigm here is the indicative mood. And since no imperative conclusion is derivable from indicative premises alone, the functional disparity between value judgments and factual judgments precludes derivation of the former from the latter. So too, it follows that value judgments lack genuine truth-value.

Even from such an abrupt survey of noncognitivism this much seems clear: Though noncognitivists neither need nor want the DMS, they are still compelled to hold that 'right' and 'ought' are ambiguous, for their description of these words is believable only in regard to sentences like i–iv, not sentences like v–viii.

(i)   Confessing your guilt was the right thing to do.

(ii)   Six months from now will be the right time to buy stocks.

(iii)   You ought to forgive him.

(iv)   I ought to take a vacation.

(v)   He gave the right answer to the question.

(vi)   Six o'clock is the right time now.

(vii)   The roast ought to be done by now.

(viii)   This piece of news ought to come as no surprise to you.

Thus, noncognitivists are committed to what I shall call the Doctrine of Practical Senses (hereafter, DPS). This is the thesis that 'right' and 'ought' (and perhaps other words) have (at least) two senses: a practical sense (as in i–iv), and a nonpractical sense (as in v–viii).

Like the DMS, the DPS needs a criterion demarcating the uses correlated to the different senses. Something analogous to the M-criterion is required. By extrapolating from the remarks of two advocates of the DPS, Castañeda and Gauthier, a crude criterion can be constructed.*

The word "ought" is ambiguous. But in some of its meanings it is part of assertions which belong typically to the language of action. . . . An ought-assertion is practical or belongs essentially to the language of action if it is proffered somehow with the purpose of making, or guiding somebody else's choice of persons, objects, or actions.[16]

Let us attempt a general statement of the difference between the use of 'ought' . . . in practical judgment and in conditional prediction. In a practical judgment, the conclusion rests on reasons for acting; in a conditional prediction, it rests on reasons for an occurrence of an event.[17]

As they stand, these remarks are unfit as a criterion since they are phrased in terms of illocutions, not sentences in which the word appears. (Why that unfits them will be explained later.) However, they invite the construction of a criterion along the following lines.

---

* No suggestion that these writers are noncognitivists is intended. Just as the DMS is not an exclusively intuitionistic doctrine, the DPS is not an exclusively noncognitivistic doctrine.

The Philosophical Context

First, a few terms need to be introduced. I call an illocution *practical* if its principal point is to guide conduct, or something very much like that. I call an illocution *declarative* if it possesses a truth-value. I call a sentence *associable with* a certain kind of illocution if utterances of sentences of that type characteristically are, or are intended to be, illocutions of that kind, and are so because of the semantic and syntactic structures of the sentence. Thus, 'Hello.' is associable with greetings, but 'How are you?' is not; 'I promise to do it.' is associable with promises, but 'I'll do it.' is not. Similarly, sentence-environments can be associable with a certain kind of illocution: 'I warn you that _____' is associable with warnings. Finally, I shall say that a word in a sentence is a *determinative of* that sentence's having some property if deleting the word or replacing it with some other word can produce a meaningful sentence lacking that property. In the sentence 'I promise to bring the red book.', 'promise' is and 'red' is not a determinative of that sentence's being associable with promises. Given all this, I shall say that *a word is being used practically* if and only if the word is a determinative of the sentence's being associable with practical illocutions, and not merely, if at all, associable with declarative illocutions. I call this the P-criterion.

Obviously the P-criterion is crude and clumsy; the definitions of the key terms are slapdash expedients. Still, it suffices; it captures what noncognitivists have in mind without begging the central question of the DPS. That is, the P-criterion leaves open whether two different senses correspond to the two sets of uses. It leaves unprejudiced the step leading to the DPS, then on to noncognitivism, namely that of imputing to a word or sentence the properties of the illocutions associable with the sentence in which the word appears. The move is a natural one for noncognitivists, because they tend to treat what they call a separate *use* of a word as constituting or correlating with a separate *sense* of the word. As with the DMS, the meaning of a word (or sentence) is conflated with what the speaker who utters it means. However, the DMS confuses the meaning of a word in a sentence with some feature of the reasons the speaker would give or accept in support of his utterance of the sentence, whereas the DPS identifies it with the speech act and correlative illocution that the speaker intends to be performing or producing in uttering the sentence.

The treatment of illocutionary properties as word or sentence properties is exemplified in the noncognitivists' mapping of the relation of 'right' and 'ought' onto imperatives. Much of their investigation is marred by inattention to the ambiguity of the term 'imperative', which refers either to a sentence mood or to an illocution. Both the investigation and the inattention largely stem from Hare, who contrasts imperatives with indicatives and leaves his reader to assume that he is consistently referring to kinds of grammatical moods. Yet, in the very heart of Hare's theory, he places three propositions, which, if he is not equivocating, are incompatible.

(!) "No imperative conclusion can be validly drawn from a set of premises which does not contain at least one imperative." [18]

(!!) Value judgments (i.e., sentences such as 'N ought to X' and 'X is right' when used evaluatively [i.e., such that they entail an imperative]) entail an imperative. (I.e., An imperative conclusion can be validly drawn from a set of premises which contains at least one value judgment.) [19]

(!!!) Value judgments are not imperatives; they are indicatives.[20]

Proposition !! is the substance of Hare's conclusion. Proposition ! is his major premise; it is supposed to be a linguistic principle a violation of which is a commission of the naturalistic fallacy. Proposition !!! is uninteresting but true, and contradicts the conjunction of ! and !!. If "imperative" and "indicative" are meant to refer to syntactical structures, Hare is refuting ! with !! and !!!. Actually, Hare offers an analysis of these syntactical notions in functional (i.e., illocutionary) terms, an analysis which alters them in such a way that !!! would be false because of the illocutionary function of value judgments. But now, how is Hare to *prove*, as he wants to, that a practical illocution cannot be, or be derivable from, a declarative illocution? * He cannot appeal to ! as a premise, for in terms of his analysis that premise *is* that conclusion. And he cannot defend ! by appeal to existing syntactic structures, for they have been set aside. Hare can only appeal to his proposed syntactic structures which are intended to reflect the illocutionary function of utterances, but since those structures are built around proposition !, they stand or fall with it and cannot support it. However all this may be, it is evident that if we are to apply the P-criterion we need to get a few things straight about the relations between the imperative mood, practical illocutions, and 'right' and 'ought.'

In general, sentences in the imperative mood are associable with practical illocutions. The very notion of grammatical mood is probably parasitic upon the idea that sentences of different forms serve different speech functions. In any case, the classification of sentences by mood is done with purely grammatical criteria (in the grammarian's sense of 'grammatical'). In consequence, being in the imperative mood is neither necessary nor sufficient for being associable with practical illocutions.

---

* Cf.: "If we admit, as I shall later maintain, that it must be part of the function of a moral judgment to prescribe or guide choices . . . then it is clear, from [proposition !], that no moral judgment can be a pure statement of fact." [21]

The Significance of Sense

An indicative sentence like 'I command you to do it.' is associable with practical illocutions (i.e., commands), and so are 'It's your turn to move.' and 'I wouldn't do that if I were you.'. Imperative sentences like 'Go screw yourself!', 'Damn it!', 'Castle and you mate in ten moves.', and 'Let it rain, let it storm! (What do I care; I've got my love to keep me warm.)' have no clear connection to guiding action.

Now, the sole reason for thinking that sentences containing 'ought' or 'right' are in the imperative mood is that some categorical indicative sentences containing 'right 'or 'ought' are like imperative sentences in being associable with practical illocutions. But that is no reason at all; it is self-defeating because of the stipulation that the senences be indicatives. Without that stipulation one would have the truly insane proposition that sentences like 'Ought I to leave now?' are *really* imperatives.

'Ought' is especially unfit for use in the imperative mood. Since 'ought' is a modal auxiliary verb it cannot be the initial word of a noninterrogative sentence, and thus cannot form an imperative as nonauxiliary verbs can.* Sentences containing 'ought' are genuine imperatives only when 'ought' appears in a noninitial clause: 'Give him what you ought to give him!'. Of course, 'right' fits easily into imperative sentences ('Come at the right time!'), but so does any other adjective. Anyway, sentence mood has little to do with word meaning except for

---

* Possible exceptions to this are exclamations like, "Will you look at that boy dance!', and 'Could you but see her now!'. The former is a degenerate interrogative. The latter is derived from a hypothetical indicative by inversion of the modal and deletion of 'if' and optional deletion of the apodosis: 'If you could but see her now, _____. The latter transformation is common with 'should' ('Should anyone call while I'm out, take a message.'), but in such cases 'should' is the conditional form of 'shall', not a synonym of 'ought'.

some oddities like 'whoa'. Unless 'ought' means the same in 'Ought I to leave now?' and 'You ought to leave now.' the latter would not serve as an answer to the former. (See pp. 44–45.)

Finally, the relation between 'ought' and 'right' and practical illocutions needs examination. I shall confine myself to plotting the uses of 'ought' which are practical according to the P-criterion. Only a tiny fraction of the sentence-environments 'ought' can appear in are associable with practical illocutions. Here are some sentences that are *not* so associable: 'I wonder if you ought to do it.', 'To tell someone what he ought to do is not to tell him to do it.', 'Whenever you ought to call your mother you get constipated.', 'The realization that I ought to be courteous has little effect on my behavior.'. Even sentences like 'He (they, Jones) ought to do it.' are not usually used to produce genuine practical illocutions since they are spoken to the wrong person for them to be action-guiding. For that matter, sentences like 'I ought to do it.' are, in general, produced as practical illocutions only when the speaker is muttering to himself—hardly the central use of such sentences.

Furthermore, though many 'ought' sentences are associable with practical illocutions, 'ought' is usually not a determinative of the sentence's having that property: 'Give him what you ought to give him.', 'Even if you ought to do it, I'm not going to let you.', 'You need not do as you ought.'. As far as I can see, in only one kind of sentence is 'ought' clearly a determinative of the sentence's being clearly associable with practical illocutions, namely: *noun or pronoun phrase referring to the audience* ought (not) to *verb phrase naming some human action*. But though 'ought' is a determinative of sentences of this form being associable with practical illocutions, so are the rest of the sentence components. So, it is not a word, but a sentence-environment that is associable with practical illocutions. Put it a different way: According to the P-criterion, in general, 'ought' is being used practically only when the speaker is telling his audience *what* they ought to do, or *that* they ought to do it, or that *they* ought to do it. (All these kinds of telling are done with the same sentences.) So it seems that precious few of the uses of 'ought' are practical.

But all this may lead noncognitivists to reject the P-criterion as being unfaithful to their conception of the practical uses of a word. They might insist that 'ought' is being used practically whenever its subject refers to an agent and its verb phrase refers to a human action.* Call this the P_o-criterion. No doubt it is better than the P-criterion at capturing all the cases non-cognitivists want to call practical uses, since (one hopes) they do not suppose that 'ought' shifts its sense in this speech: 'Yesterday I was uncertain about who ought to tackle this job. But now that I've met you, my mind is made up. *You* ought to do it.'. Unhappily, the P-criterion, not the P_o-criterion, provides the leverage for what non-cognitivists want to say about the practical uses, because the former does, while the latter does not, link the uses of 'ought' to particular illocutions and thereby suggest a semantic split. (This whole discussion is reproducible with 'right' in place of 'ought'.)

What is the source of the difficulty here? I suggest that, just as the intuitionists' DMS is a semantic version of the Kantian categorical-hypothetical imperative distinction, the noncognitivists' DPS is a semantic correlate of the Aristotelian distinction

---

* Other things besides actions might be included—e.g., 'You ought to be ashamed of yourself.'. Even so, this criterion won't do. Cf.: 'We ought to arrive soon. We've been walking for half an hour and the place is only two miles from where we started.'.

between the practical and the theoretical, between determining what to do and determining what is the case.* The traditional distinction is not unproblematic, partly because of unclarities about the nature of the conclusion of a practical syllogism—is it a proposition? A belief? A decision? An action? But whatever its defects, at least the traditional distinction was not cast as involving a semantic distinction; that is a noncognitivist innovation. Noncognitivists conceive of morality as being directed toward answering the question 'What shall I do?',[22] and construe the philosophical problems as linguistic ones. Thus, they focus on the use of language at the nexus of argument and action. Then, because of their linguistic theory, they find it natural to account for the logic of the decision-making process by importing features of the speech context into the meanings of certain supposedly central words. Thus the P-criterion. But, in consequence, their description of the use of these words fits comfortably only in those contexts. In order to account for the other logical relations those words have, the use of those words must be liberated from the special speech contexts. Thus the P_o-criterion. But that criterion marks a difference in the topics of discourse without suggesting a difference in the semantics of the discourse itself. (See Chapter Three.)

Up to this point I have concentrated on specifying the practical uses of 'right' and 'ought'. But now, does any special meaning attach to these words in this set of uses? Two characterizations of the practical sense of 'ought' have won some

---

* Alternatively, the noncognitivist is a skeptical intuitionist; to him, for moral language and morality to be possible there must be things that, though they may be in this world, are not of this world—but he cannot believe in such things. (See Wittgenstein's "Lecture on Ethics.") Of course, on the other hand intuitionists are wont to interpret noncognitivism as a species of subjectivistic naturalism.

fame, so I shall quickly review them. Other characterizations are possible. No matter, for my defense of the univocity of 'ought' and 'right' does not work by some process of elimination. And as for the nonpractical sense, I know of no philosophical characterizations.

According to Hare, an 'ought' judgment (in the "evaluative sense" of 'ought') entails an imperative; 'I ought to do X' entails 'Let me do X'.[23] According to Nowell-Smith, 'I ought to do X' entails 'I shall do X'.[24] * These contentions presuppose that, in its practical use, 'ought' is an "action-guiding word", that an agent's belief that he ought to do X has some necessary connection with his intending to do X. Both writers are faced with the phenomenon of *akrasia*, but they face it in different ways. Since Hare defines his evaluative sense of 'ought' in terms of its entailing an imperative, he must show that the word has such a sense. It is a problem without a solution.

Nowell-Smith tries to escape by arguing that 'ought' entails 'shall' in the intentional, but not in the predictive sense of 'shall'. This is little different from Hare's situation, for there is no non–question-begging way of showing that only the predictive sense is not entailed. However, Nowell-Smith's move has an added interest for us, because he is defending his version of the DPS regarding 'ought' by appealing to another popular [25] instance of the DPS, this time regarding 'shall'. And as with 'ought', the idea that 'shall' has a practical (intentional) and a nonpractical (predictive) sense is due to a confusion of the properties of an illocution with the meaning of a word. This is of special relevance here, since 'shall' and its near synonym 'will',

---

* It is worth stating here, though not worth arguing about until Chapter Three, that both of these contentions exhibit the prevalent philosophical confusion of 'ought' with 'must'.

like 'ought' and its synonym 'should', belong to the small and distinctive grammatical class of modal auxiliary verbs. Because it is a trait common to such verbs to be a determinative of a sentence's having multiple illocutionary potential, I want to scotch the idea that 'shall' is ambiguous.

Again, 'shall' is thought to be ambiguous because it is a determinative of the sentence-environment 'I shall VP', being associable with predictions and expressions of intention, illocutions having different truth conditions. Let us write 'shall$_i$' for the intentional uses of 'shall' and 'shall$_p$' for the predictive uses. Then, 'I shall$_p$ sing.' is true if and only if I sing at some time after my utterance. Not so with 'I shall$_i$ sing.', for it lacks a full-fledged truth-value altogether. For note, 'I shall$_i$ sing.' does not mean 'I intend to sing.'. The latter is true if and only if I have a certain intention, that of singing, and if I lack it, then 'I intend to sing.' is false, but 'I shall$_i$ sing.' is not. To be sure, if I say 'I shall$_i$ sing.' and you discover that I have no intention of singing, then you can charge me with lying—not because I said something false, but because I knowingly misled you. And if I have the intention and say 'I intend to sing.', you can say of me, 'He's telling the truth.'. One does not say that of me if I say 'I shall$_i$ sing.'. Instead one might say 'He really means it.'. In brief, whereas 'I intend to VP' is used to *state* an intention, 'I shall$_i$ VP' is not; it is used to *express* an intention.

Note also, 'I shall$_p$ VP' does not mean 'I predict that I will VP'. Again, 'I shall$_p$ sing.' is true if and only if I sing at some time after my utterance; not so with 'I predict that I will sing.', for (if it has a truth-value at all) it is true if and only if I predict that I will sing. To be sure, if I say 'I predict that I will sing.' and I do (not) sing, then I can be said to have been right (mistaken)—not because I said something true (false), but because, by saying what I said, I conversationally implicate * that I *believed* something would happen which, as it turns out, does (not) happen.

Now if 'I shall$_i$ VP' had the truth conditions of 'I intend to VP' or if 'I shall$_p$ VP' had the truth conditions of 'I predict that I will VP', then maybe the DPS could gain entrance. But as things stand, the DPS is gratuitous here, for it is wholly natural that 'I shall VP' have both functions, since they are related and similar. One says 'I shall$_i$ VP' when agreeing, warning, threatening, promising, and similar things. To do such things is not to *predict* that an act will occur, but to *guarantee* it. That is, the *point* of saying 'I shall$_i$ sing.' is to give grounds for believing that 'I shall$_p$ sing.' is true. (Note that warning and similar acts are also performed with 'I shall$_p$ VP'.) † Though 'I intend to VP' serves many of these functions, it does so more derivatively than 'I shall$_i$ VP'; in its most immediate interpretation, 'I intend to VP' serves to report a present state of the speaker, not to guarantee the future occurrence of an act. Note that 'I intend to do it but I may fail.' makes perfect sense, but 'I shall do it but I may fail.' makes no sense at all.

The DPS is gratuitous here because 'shall' indicates futur-

---

* The phrase 'conversationally implicate' and the theory in which it operates were devised by H. P. Grice. His terminology and the greater part of his theory have yet to appear in print. However, sections 2–4 of his essay, "The Casual Theory of Perception" present enough of his theory for present purposes.

† When I predict I *let you take* my word for it; when I guarantee I *give you* my word on it—sometimes the very same word as when I predict. (Cf. Austin's discussion of 'know' and 'promise'.[26]) I am not saying 'I shall$_i$ VP' is always used to guarantee, nor that 'I shall$_p$ VP' is always used to predict. Rather I am pointing to a continuum of closely related illocutions.

ity,* and thus it is wholly natural that 'I shall VP' should be associable with predicting and guaranteeing the performance of an act. More, the DPS is not merely gratuitous; it is paradoxical. If the dual illocutionary function of 'I shall VP' implies that 'shall' is ambiguous, then 'will', 'won't', 'shan't', 'am going to', 'am about to', and the bound morpheme ''ll' must also be similarly ambiguous. For that matter, virtually every verb in the English language that can take an agent for a subject must be ambiguous since they can form sentences like 'I leave tomorrow.' which are associable with both predictions and expressions of intention. Surely no level-headed lexicographer would think that a reason for doubling the dictionary entries of every such verb.

But let us stick with 'shall'. Consider the following conversation:

J: We shall meet again some day. I'm sure of it.
K: Well, I certainly hope that we shall (meet again some day).
L: Don't worry, we shall (meet again some day). I firmly intend that we shall (meet again some day).

J is predicting, K is expressing a hope, and L is expressing an intention. Does each utterance of 'we shall meet again someday' mean something different? If so, it will be something of a mystery how J can be predicting what K is hoping for and L is intending. They are all talking about the same thing: their meeting again at some future time.

----

* I am not saying what 'shall' means or that it is univocal over *all* its uses. My concern is only with the claim that it is ambiguous in the environment 'I shall VP' and that this is shown by that environment's having multiple illocutionary potential.

The Significance of Sense

Finally, take a genuinely ambiguous word: 'ball'. The sentence-frame 'X is a ball and X is not a ball' can be given an interpretation which is not self-contradictory: 'X is a gala dance and X is not a spheroid object'. If 'shall' were ambiguous in the environment 'I _____ VP', then 'I shall VP and I shall not VP' would have a non–self-contradictory interpretation. But it is inescapably self-contradictory. It is not merely odd as is 'I believe it is raining and it isn't.'. Moore's paradox is odd in virtue of certain conversational implicatures. But 'I shall VP and I shall not VP' is self-contradictory just as is 'I leave tomorrow and I do not leave tomorrow.'. By contrast, 'I intend to VP and I shall not VP' and 'I predict that I will VP and I shall not VP' may be odd in the way that Moore's paradox is odd, but they are not self-contradictory.*

So much for the DPS regarding 'shall', and regarding 'ought' and 'right' as well. This ends my survey of noncognitivism and intuitionism. If the conclusions of this chapter seem ill-supported, that is at least partly due to a lack of premises, a deficiency that subsequent chapters are designed to repair. I have said little about naturalism, and shall not say much more. I shall not propound or defend any substantive naturalistic theory except in some obiter dicta lying to the side of my central argument on the univocity of 'right' and 'ought'.† My

---

* Note that all my arguments ultimately rest on our linguistic intuitions. This is unavoidable. To undermine one linguistic intuition we must appeal to other incompatible intuitions. Given a conflict in immediate linguistic intuitions the problem then becomes one of theory construction. (See Chapter Two.)

† N.B.: My claim that 'ought' and 'right' are univocal is stronger than the denial of the DMS and DPS in regard to 'ought' and 'right'. The stronger claim rules out other possible ambiguist theses such as that 'right' is heterotypically ambiguous.

accounts of these words are compatible with any substantive naturalistic theory or, for that matter, any ethical theory at all, even radical skepticism. My conclusions oppose only meta-ethical theories. This is of some importance. It is sometimes said that meta-ethics cannot be ethically neutral. I think that is true, but only of bad meta-ethics. I think meta-ethics is like astronomy: in its more primitive forms all sorts of fraudulent claims about human affairs are derived, but in its more developed form it is silent on such subjects. It has also been said, this time by more radical opponents of linguistically oriented schools of philosophy, that meta-ethics is an acarpous enterprise. I am in sympathy with that judgment, though generally not with the biases from which it springs. I think philosophers have been doing the wrong thing because they do it badly, and therefore in this case only a thief can catch the thief.

Two

Counting Meanings

> We need more of a framework in which to discuss these uses of language.
>
> —J. L. Austin, "Performative Utterances"

I WANT to prove that 'ought' and 'right' are univocal; I want to convince my readers that this is so. But even supposing that it is so, it is far from obvious *how* I can go about proving it or *whether* it can be proven at all. So, some things need to be learned—and some need to be unlearned—before my arguments in subsequent chapters can be assessed. However, little originality can be claimed for most of this chapter, since it is largely an application to the problem of ambiguity of results previously established in other areas.

In general it is not difficult to get unanimous assent from intelligent native speakers as to whether some word or sentence is ambiguous, or whether two different words are synonymous, or whether two tokens of the same word-type are being used in the same sense. If this were not so, maybe language would be impossible. But sometimes unanimity is not achieved immediately. Often upon hearing a sentence one thinks of only one of its interpretations and must be reminded of the other possible reading(s). Upon hearing the sentence 'I saw a shark.', one might (I did) think of 'shark' as meaning only a kind of fish and need to be reminded that it also means a kind of man. In general, after the reminder the disagreement will cease. (Of course, one might need to be *told* the facts. A student of mine had consistently mis-heard the phrases 'loan shark', 'pool shark', as 'loan sharp', 'pool sharp'.)

Sometimes, even after the purported ambiguities have been pointed out, the disagreement continues. It may persist even between two intelligent, competent native speakers trained in the study of language and having highly sensitive ears. For instance, Ziff [1] believes that 'Someone was a child.' is not synonymous with 'Someone was a parent.'. I agree, but Chomsky, Katz, and Martin [2] do not. It might be said that this disagreement is more over the notion of synonymity than over the meanings of each of the sentences, but it would be better to say that those two kinds of disagreements are not always sharply separable. Anyway, there are other actual or possible disagreements. For example, Richard Hare thinks that 'right' and 'ought' are ambiguous, and I do not.

The question then arises: What rational procedures can be used to settle an ambiguity dispute, i.e., a disagreement in the linguistic intuitions of two competent, intelligent native speakers over whether some word or sentence in their language is ambiguous? That is not an easy question; a complete answer would be tantamount to an adequate linguistic theory. (Conversely, such a theory is difficult to construct, partly because differences in linguistic intuitions put much of the crucial data in doubt.) If that is true, then different linguistic theories will probably provide different answers to the question.

The Significance of Sense

The answer given by Richman in "Ambiguity and Intuition" is that ambiguity disputes cannot be settled by rational procedures. In brief, he contends that for any term P, one can say either that its extension is the two classes A and B or some single class of which A and B are subclasses. In the latter case the extension may be simply the union of A and B. The decision to treat the extension as one or as many classes is arbitrary and thus so is the decision as to whether the word is univocal or ambiguous.

Richman's argument does not, as apparently intended, present a general difficulty for ambiguity disputes, since it is inapplicable unless an extension is assignable to both of the senses. The argument fails with a word like 'round' which is both a preposition and an adjectve, since as a preposition, it cannot sensibly be said to have an extension at all.* More broadly, the argument fails because it largely begs the question by assuming without proof that the only relevant considerations are straightforward extensional ones.

Further, his conclusion is unjustified even when only extensional considerations are available. His article ends by confessing that if the extension is composed of two or more sets containing radically different kinds of members (e.g., 'bat'), it would be implausible to treat them as subclasses of the same class. But, he says, it is just as much a matter of intuition whether two properties or their classes of instances are radically different as whether a word is ambiguous. Even supposing that this latter claim is correct (and it is questionable), and thus

---

* It might be contended that there are two words here, not one ambiguous word. For some purposes that division is useful; here it is not. If we say there are two words, the question is whether they are synonymous. If we say there is one word, the question is whether it is univocal. I am using phonetic-ideographic identity within one language as the criterion for word-identity.

36

supposing that *at some point* in an ambiguity dispute one must appeal to intuitions, it does not follow that the final decision is arbitrary. If nothing else, one has moved to a different intuition which may or may not result in agreement. Richman might claim that one cannot form an argument—at least not a conclusive argument—by using premises that are open to doubt and disagreement in much the same way and to the same extent as the conclusion. Some such claim seems implicit in his article, but any such claim is false. Compare: You and I have normal eyesight but we disagree on the color of an object we are examining. In an attempt to settle our dispute we take the object out of our fluorescent-lit room into the sunlight of a cloudless day. We may still disagree—but then again, we may not. It would be odd to call this procedure or its result arbitrary.

Richman is hardly alone in his position on disputes over ambiguity; quite the contrary, he is in distinguished company. Note Quine's response to those philosophers maintaining that 'true' and 'exist' are ambiguous: "What mainly baffles me is the stoutness of their maintenance. What can they possibly count as evidence?" [3]

Here, as in many other areas, Wittgenstein is Quine's ally. Wittgenstein writes:

There can be two kinds of discussions as to whether a word is used in one way or in two ways: (a) Two people may discuss whether the English word "cleave" is only used for chopping up something or also for joining things together. This is a discussion about the facts of a certain actual usage. (b) They may discuss whether the word "altus", standing for both "deep" and "high", is *thereby* used in two different ways. This question is analogous to the question whether the word "thought" is used in two ways or in one when we talk of conscious and unconscious thoughts. The man who says "surely, there are two different usages" has already decided to use a two-way schema, and what he said expressed that decision.[4]

It is of such decisions to say one thing rather than another that Wittgenstein says, "Either form of expression is correct; but they may betray different tendencies of the mind." [5]

Quine and Wittgenstein do not formulate specific arguments sustaining their position. They do not need to, for their position is a consequence of their semantic theories and their conception of the nature of meaning, a conception which they largely share. And, as the son is like the father, my conception of meaning is much like theirs. Yet, I reject their position on ambiguity. I do so because I think our (their and my) conception of meaning is one in terms of which rational procedures can be devised for settling such disputes.

The fundamental tenet of this philosophy of language is that linguistic meaning is a function solely of the behavior of the speakers of the language. It is not necessary to suppose that words are used according to what are properly called rules; one need suppose only that there are describable regularities in the use of a word. On this basis one can treat an account of a word as a lower-order scientific theory. An account of a word is a description of the salient facts about the use of the word (e.g., its semantic and syntactic relations) in a simple, comprehensive, and accurate manner. The principal data are the judgments that competent native speakers make about utterances in which the word appears (and utterances related to such utteraces) as well as the utterances themselves. Of primary interest are their judgments as to the grammaticality of such utterances and their appropriateness in various contexts.*

---

* Of course, speakers may disagree in their judgments on these matters independently of disagreements over ambiguity. Sometimes disagreement is spurious; one party retracts upon serious reflection. Sometimes

Counting Meanings

From such relatively unimpeachable data, a hypothesis about the behavior of the word can be formulated. (Of course, this presupposes that one already has at least crude tentative hypotheses about the semantic and syntactic structures of the language.) And since one never examines each of the unlimited number of utterances in which the word can appear, the hypothesis can be tested for its ability to predict the grammaticality and appropriateness of the word in as yet unexamined utterances and speech contexts.

By so treating an account of a word, the objections of Wittgenstein and Quine can be met, since competing scientific theories are assessable by rational procedures. To be sure, the criteria of assessment may not be strong or complete or precise enough to enable us to judge all but one theory to be inadequate. It may be, as Quine and perhaps Wittgenstein think, that there can be no such thing as the one and only correct scientific theory. Even if that is true, it says no more about theories of discourse than it does about theories of disease. Thus it seems misleading to emphasize the subjectivistic aspects of the problem of ambiguity.

As in the physical sciences, various considerations can be used to evaluate competing theories (accounts). Permitting while not possessing disconfirmation is one important asset of a theory, but it is not the only one. If it were, then it would often and perhaps always be impossible to make a nonarbitrary choice between competing ambiguist and univocalist accounts. Thus, though naturally I think my accounts "fit the facts", it is not on that basis that I claim them to be preferable to any ambig-

---

the disagreement persists and must be attributed to genuine linguistic divergence. I shall be supposing that there is or upon reflection would be unanimity in the judgments of grammaticality and appropriateness, and I shall use this data to show that 'ought' and 'right' are univocal.

uist account. So let us look at some other considerations.

Just as with scientific theories, the simpler of two accounts is preferable, all other things being roughly equal. Considerations of simplicity provide a ground for appealing to a linguistic analogue of Occam's Razor: don't multiply senses beyond necessity. (Ziff calls this "Occam's eraser".[6]) More precisely, a univocalist account is preferable to a competing ambiguist account unless other considerations make the ambiguist account preferable. In other words, *ceteris paribus*, a univocalist account is preferable to an ambiguist account.

However, Occam's eraser may seem to be of only academic interest in connection with my account of 'ought', for, though it is univocalist, it is also quite complex; many pages are required just to explain the definition, let alone defend it. One might conclude that a univocalist account of 'ought' must be far more complex than an ambiguist account. But the complexity of my account results not from its being univocalist, but from its being noncircular. If accuracy, simplicity, and elegance were all that were required, a univocalist definition would win hands down: 'Ought' means the same as 'should' where 'should' is not a past or conditional form of 'shall'. That definition would be flawless were it not that it is fruitless (at least for present purposes). A useful definition of 'ought' will require certain complexities—which may or may not be the ones I chose.* And, I might add, I don't much care whether my univocalist accounts of 'right' and 'ought' are the simplest or the best possible. What matters here is that a univocalist account of these words is preferable to an ambiguist account.

Two other considerations are worth mentioning. First, one

---

* Any account of 'ought' ought to be complex enough to explain how and why the word has inspired so much debate. An account that was too simple should inspire suspicion.

theory (account) is preferable to another if it is more in harmony with accepted theories and with the procedures and principles which are essential to the higher-order theories and the science to which they belong. That is, a theory should fit not only the facts, but also other accepted theories. Whole sections of Chapters Three and Four are written with this in mind. Secondly, one theory is preferable to another if it is more powerful or general. A theory is to be preferred if it accounts for all of, but not only, the facts accounted for by its competitors. It is therefore of some importance that my account of 'ought' is only one part of a unified account of virtually the whole modal auxiliary system of English.

In consequence of such considerations the preferred theory often runs counter to many common-sense beliefs. For example, the Copernican theory conflicts with what looks like the undeniable evidence of the senses. Every day we see the sun "move" across the sky from east to west, and we are quite familiar with the experience of being on a moving object, but it doesn't look or feel as though we are on one all our lives. And it is also a familiar fact of experience that an object that is on, but unattached to, a moving object soon falls off. Copernicus could overcome such formidable evidence only by appealing to other evidence that was also, in complex ways, based on common sense and sense experience.

Our sense of ambiguity is no more infallible than our sense of motion. Admittedly, the intuition of most native speakers (I have sampled them) is that 'ought' and 'right' are ambiguous, and, after all, a language is what the native speakers of the language speak, and surely they must know what they mean by the words they speak. All this is true, but inconclusive; that my claim is counter-intuitive is objectionable, but not fatally so. We have two criteria for knowing the meaning of a word (and thus knowing whether the word is ambiguous): being able to use the word correctly (e.g., knowing what are grammatical and appropriate uses of the word) and being able to explain the meaning of the word (e.g., being able to give a definition). These are not totally independent abilities, but in any particular case neither is a prerequisite of the other. That a language is what its native speakers speak ensures that the intuitions of native speakers on the correctness of a use of a word are, in general, the court of last resort. That the speakers unavoidably know what they mean ensures that they are experts at explaining the meaning of a word—but it does not ensure that they are infallible, and would not ensure it unless *what* they mean were some private mental entity which they wish to inspire in others by their use of language. The trouble is not that speakers know but can't say the meaning (i.e., they haven't hit upon a happy formulation), but that the meaning of a word is a function of their behavior, their exercise of their own linguistic competence. So, to state the meaning of a word is to hypothesize about the exercise of linguistic competence, not to report on an article of inner experience. In consequence, our intuitions of meaning, synonymy, and ambiguity are expert testimony on the subject, but not an infallible guide. Yet common sense can be overthrown only bit by bit, not altogether in an instant. The only way I can undermine the initial intuitions about 'right' and 'ought' is by appealing to other linguistic intuitions and the requirements of an adequate account. Of course, if most native speakers lack these intuitions then I am bereft of argument, and must be dismissed as a linguistic deviant.*

Much of this was illustrated by my discussion of 'shall'. To

---

* This whole discussion bears on the psychiatrist's claim to confute the patient's report of his own intentions and motives.

large numbers of philosophers, linguists, and untrained native speakers it has seemed obvious that 'shall' has a predictive and an intentional sense. I discredited this more or less common-sense belief by appealing to other beliefs which either are or are based on common-sense beliefs. And at one point I implicitly appealed to a principle based on the need for conservatism in overthrowing common sense. (It is also based on Occam's eraser and the requirement of consistency.) I call this principle Putman's rule, after Hilary Putnam, who suggested it to me. However, I am not (though Putnam may be) very clear about how to state this rule precisely. Roughly, the idea is that we ought to reject any purported linguistic principle whose consistent application compels us to deem ambiguous a large class of words which it would be counter-intuitive to deem ambiguous. On this basis I contended that the fact that 'I shall VP' can be either a prediction or an expression of intention is no reason for calling 'shall' ambiguous, for if it were, then virtually every verb that can take an agent for a subject would be deemed ambiguous.

Because I treat an account of a word as a scientific theory one should not expect, and I shall not offer, knockdown, a priori arguments starting from indubitable premises and proceeding to equally indubitable conclusions.* Naturally I think that my conclusions are true and that my premises are more obviously true than the conclusions. But I may be mistaken. That is an occupational hazard of science—especially in contemporary linguistics. For note that the application of the principles of theory assessment, and thus the preference for a particular

---

* As such, my procedure contrasts with the usual practice of meta-ethicists. Too often they seem to treat the determination of a word's meaning as an a priori problem instead of an empirical one.

theory are largely determined by already accepted theories. The premises on which one argues for a new theory are, in the main, the results of previous research that has received widespread acceptance. But, in part because linguistics is a relatively young science, disagreement on fundamental issues is common, and thus, generally accepted theories on which to base one's claims are rare. (Compounding my own difficulties, I lack a mastery of much that is widely accepted by linguists.)

All this has consequences for my accounts and their defense. In essence, my thesis is that one takes 'right' and 'ought' to be ambiguous only because one imports into the meaning of the words certain matters that don't belong there. So I need to prove that my explanation of the linguistic facts is preferable to one invoking a shift in meaning. But in the metaphysician's (as opposed to the scientist's) sense of 'proof', I can't prove it, for in that sense I need at least a virtually complete linguistic theory before I can even begin. And though the scientist makes milder (and more realistic) demands, I cannot, if only for lack of space, meet even them.

Let me illustrate this last point with a simple-minded example. Earlier I declared that sentence mood has little to do with word meaning. In support of this claim I said: "Unless 'ought' means the same in 'Ought I to leave now?' as it does in 'You ought to leave now.' the latter would not serve as an answer to the former." That is not a rigorous argument: The premise is neither unquestionable nor sufficient to establish the conclusion. But a rigorous proof of that claim would require a separate essay, and I need to make many such claims before I can reach my conclusions about 'ought' and 'right'. Furthermore, for many of these claims I *could not*—nor could anyone else— now provide a rigorous proof.

Nevertheless, linguistics is not so unformed as to preclude

intelligent projections about the general form that linguistic descriptions should take. Enough is known to allow some fairly blunt assertions. Take the above premise. Now perhaps there could be a language in which a word like 'ought' is ambiguous over an indicative and a correlative interrogative sentence—but English is not that language. And perhaps there could be a linguistic description of English according to which 'ought' is ambiguous over indicatives and interrogatives—but a little thought will reveal that such a description would be unnatural and unnecessary since it requires a rococo system of syntactical transformations and a network of systematic ambiguities. It should be—and I assume it is—obvious that it is far simpler, more perspicuous, and more in line with our sense of the language to describe the relations between the indicative and the correlative interrogative in terms of a constancy in the meaning and reference of the constituent terms and some simple syntactical relations.

I have said that one thinks 'ought' and 'right' are ambiguous because of confusions about what is properly part of word meaning. The DMS and DPS are two examples of such confusion. It is quite understandable why people are inclined to import various things into the meanings of words. It is natural to think of words as being the elementary components of language; and the most prominent characteristic of words is the possession of a meaning. So one's first impulse may be to try to explain the enormous variety of linguistic facts in terms of the meanings of the elementary constituents. All this is understandable, but is no longer excusable. Thanks to the genuine contributions of philosophers and linguists it has become clear that word meaning must be distinguished from other factors which play a role in our use of language.

Word meaning must be distinguished from reference, and

both must be distinguished from sentence meaning, since the meaning of a sentence is also a function of syntactical relations. In addition, the meaning of an expression (word, phrase, or sentence) must be distinguished from the meaning of an utterance (the uttered expression), since the latter is a function also of what the speaker means. And all these must be distinguished from the speech act and the perlocutionary and illocutionary forces of the utterance, for they are a function also of the circumstances in which the expression is uttered. And all these must be distinguished from what the speaker implies by his uttering of the expression and what his uttering of the expression implies, for such implications are a function also of general rules of conversation. And all these, especially the meaning of an expression, must be distinguished from deep-seated beliefs and attitudes associated with the expression (e.g., beliefs about things to which a word applies).

I am assuming that it is necessary and proper to treat expressions (words, phrases, sentences) as units of meaning that are isolable and relatively stable among a particular community over a certain stretch of time. Granted, the meaning of an expression has essential connections with the total speech act performed in uttering the expression in particular circumstances. Granted, the meaning of an expression is not logically independent of the way that speakers of the language speak and behave in general. And granted, I can mean whatever I want to mean by an expression I utter. But still, if what I utter is a grammatically well-formed expression, *it* has a meaning in the language, and has that meaning independently of anything I may do or mean on some particular occasions.

I am interested in the English words 'ought' (the modal auxiliary) and 'right' (the adjective whose antonym is 'wrong'). I am interested in their meaning or meanings as they are *now* used by most native English speakers. Primarily, I am interested in whether these words are ambiguous. And since, "If we are to understand the linguistic source of ambiguity, we must attend to the source of a sentence's potential for ambiguity," [7] I am secondarily interested in the meaning of sentences in which these words appear.

I want to present definitions of these words, but I am not concerned to present some expressions that can be paired with the definienda by our synonymy intuitions. The meaning of a word can be explained or defined in various ways; not all of them involve synonyms (not all dictionary definitions are synonyms). Those that do not are none the worse for it. There is no good reason to suppose or desire that a natural language contains a thoroughly redundant vocabulary. Not everything that can be said can be said in other words.

In general, the construction or presentation of a synonymous expression is of little value in philosophy. I could say that 'should' is a synonym of 'ought', but that would be of little value except to someone learning English. Few of my readers fit that description. Anyway, since my primary concern is with the univocity of two words, the presentation of a single synonym would not advance the discussion because the definiens might be ambiguous in just the way that the definiendum is. Moreover, an adequate definition need not correspond to the synonymy intuitions of a native speaker; certainly a philosophically fruitful definition need not so correspond. (That is, I think, the lesson to be learned from Moore's discussion of 'good'.)

I am not interested in the whole of the meanings of these words, but only in the logical properties of their meanings, the properties relevant to the role of a word in rational argumentation, to illocutionary force and the logical validity of arguments. By and large, I shall ignore matters of nuance, of subtle shadings of meaning which are significant only in the realms of style, rhetoric, and perlocutionary force. Some such distinction seems necessary, but I can only gesture toward a clarification of it by means of some examples. I would say that the meanings of the expressions 'mother-in-law' and 'spouse's mother' have the same logical properties. For one thing, these expressions are interchangeable *salva veritate* in all referentially transparent contexts. But a contemporary native speaker would—or properly could—use the latter in place of the former on relatively few occasions. At a minimum, such substitution would cause certain jokes to be even flatter than they now are; it would keep some from being jokes altogether. A quite similar relation obtains between the active and passive forms of a sentence.

Again, I am interested in the meanings of 'right' and 'ought'; I am not interested in the concept of right or the concept of ought. I doubt that any such things exist except in some special sense of 'concept' according to which to know how to use the word 'X' is to have the concept of X (in which case I would have a concept of an). Further, I am not interested in the criteria for being right or being that which ought to be. If what I shall say is correct, it would be at best misleading to speak of the criteria for being right or being that which ought to be (just as it is misleading to speak of the criteria for being true). And thus I shall not be concerned to say which things are right or ought to be. To know which things are right or ought to be, it is neither necessary nor sufficient that one be able to state the meanings of these words, though if one is convinced of some incorrect statement of their meanings one may be led to have incorrect opinions about what things are right or ought to be.

Finally, I am interested in the meanings of these words, not

Counting Meanings

in their uses. Various things can be meant (and have been by philosophers) by the phrase, 'the use of a word'. Many of them have nothing to do with the meaning of a word. Granted, in some extended sense of the word 'use', one can show that a word is ambiguous only by showing differences in the use of the word in different contexts (which may be either different sentence-environments or different total speech contexts). By noting the different implications involved in the different contexts one can distinguish and demarcate different senses. Of course, it is difficult to discover the implications, and prove that they really obtain. But, more importantly, not every such implication reveals something about the meaning of the word.

This last point is crucial. An uncritical acceptance of the Wittgensteinian slogan "The meaning of a word is its use in the language" has led many philosophers to argue as though every difference in use is a consequence of and evidence for a difference in meaning. Wittgenstein himself constantly argues that way. It is a mistake to argue that way; a mistake that has plagued contemporary philosophy. It lies at the root not only of large numbers of influential theories, but of a whole style of philosophy. (It's rather a pity that it is a mistake; if it weren't, philosophy would be so much simpler.) To illustrate the kinds of errors begotten by this mistake, I shall discuss four topics in Wittgenstein's *Philosophical Investigations*. In doing so, I employ some of the distinctions that I referred to earlier (pp. 45–46). I shall not give arguments for or explications of these distinctions since they already exist in the literature. My main purpose is to illustrate their application, utility, and importance. Wittgenstein is my target just because his writings are the source of much of the confusion and unsound argumentation to be found in the work of his successors, especially in meta-ethics.

The Significance of Sense

In Section 27, Wittgenstein is trying to undermine the picture of words as names of objects. My complaint here is directed not against his goal, but his form of argument. He presents a list of exclamations (or cries): "Water! Away! Ow! Help! Fine! No!", and then asks: "Are you still inclined to call these words 'names of objects'?". Leaving aside 'ow' which is not (contra Wittgenstein) a word, it is clear that he is confusing the meaning of a word with the speech act performed in uttering that word in certain circumstances. Perhaps none or only some (e.g., 'water') of these words could properly be called names, but there is nothing in Wittgenstein's remarks here that need or should disincline us to call all of them names—otherwise, it would be difficult not to conclude that *no* word is the name of an object. Any word that is plausibly called a name can be exclaimed, even proper names: 'Herr Wittgenstein!'. But if 'water' is a name in a statement like 'He wants water.', then it is a name in the exclamation 'Water!'. The meaning of the word is the same in both utterances; if it were not, the thirsty man's exclaiming 'Water!' would not imply and would not count as evidence for the truth of the observer's statement, 'He wants water.'.

In Section 117, Wittgenstein seems to be saying that an expression loses or changes its meaning when used in circumstances other than those in which it is characteristically used. Witness his remark: "As if the sense were an atmosphere accompanying the word, which it carried with it into every kind of application." Thus he says: "If, for example, someone says that the sentence "This is here" (whereby he points to an object in front of him) has sense for him, then he should ask himself in what special circumstances this sentence is actually said. There it does have sense." Here Wittgenstein is confusing the meaning of a sentence with the meaning of an utterance, that is, with what the speaker means by that sentence when he utters it. Suppose that while you and I are casually strolling down a street I suddenly say, 'This is here.' (whereby I point to a crack in the sidewalk in front of me). The sentence I utter does not lack sense. The sentence has a meaning, the only meaning it has in English. (It is not an ambiguous sentence.) But what *I* mean by my utterance, what I am trying to do or tell you by uttering that sentence, is wholly opaque. It looks as though I were trying to convey some information, but you have no idea what distinction I am trying to make or what statements I would be willing to contrast with my utterance. I may go on to explain what I mean. But I do not, at least if you speak English, explain what the sentence means. If you do not understand what the sentence means then my subsequent explanation will also be incomprehensible. I may say, 'I remember seeing and studying quite intently this very crack while on an acid trip, but I had completely forgotten, if in fact I ever knew, where in the city it was located.'. Such an explanation does not give a sense to or in any way alter the sense of the sentence I uttered. I have only specified the intended referents, not the meanings, of 'this' and 'here' and explained my interest in the fact that this (the crack) is here (at this location in the city).

Central to the mentalistic theories of meaning Wittgenstein criticizes is the thesis that the understanding of an utterance (or inscription or the like) must always be preceded by or involve some definite, private, mental act of interpretation. Wittgenstein extends the ordinary sense of the word 'interpretation' so as to include translating, decoding, and similar procedures. Roughly, interpreting is a procedure the point of which is to make what is interpreted (usually an utterance or inscription) more readily understandable or understandable at all by some audience.

Wittgenstein's critique is successful, but along the way he enters a stronger claim and bases it on illegitimate grounds. He does, I think, show that sometimes we understand without any *definite, private, mental act* of interpretation, but he wants to say further that sometimes we understand without any interpreting at all: "There is a way of grasping a rule which is *not an interpretation*" (Section 201). Whatever the truth of this stronger claim, his defense of it fails.

Essentially his argument is that sometimes it would be incorrect to say of someone that he had interpreted a particular utterance. From this Wittgenstein concludes that it would not be true that the person had interpreted the utterance. This argument confuses the meaning of a word ('interpreted') and sentences in which the word appears ('He interpreted the utterance.') with the conditions under which it is appropriate to utter such sentences. By uttering such a sentence one conversationally implicates that those conditions obtain. If they do not obtain, then it will be odd to utter the sentence.

Normally we would utter (it is appropriate to utter) a sentence of the form 'M interpreted X' only if one of the following conditions obtains:

(a)   M has gone through some definite act (inward or outward, it does not matter) of interpretation, such as substituting one set of sentences for another.

(b)   There is room for genuine doubt, by M or by us, as to what the correct interpretation is.

(c)   We believe that M has misinterpreted X.

Wittgenstein relies on the first condition in Section 201: "We ought to restrict the term 'interpretation' to the substitution of one expression of the rule for another." (Cf. Section 637.) The second condition is appealed to in Section 213: ". . . 'so you must have chosen *one* such interpretation'. —Not at all. A doubt was possible in certain circumstances. But that is not to say that I did doubt, or even could doubt." The third condition is not explicitly appealed to, but I suppose that he might do so. The third condition is closely related to the second since "When we interpret, we form hypotheses, which may prove false (page 212)."

These conversationally implicated conditions are not truth-conditions, and hence their nonoccurrence does not imply the falsity of the assertion that M interpreted X. But though Wittgenstein's argument is a bad one, it does not follow that his stronger claim is false. That is a separate issue requiring separate arguments.

In Section 408, Wittgenstein says: " 'I don't know whether I am in pain or not.' . . . is not a meaningful sentence (*sinvoller Satz*)." Page 221 suggests that he would extend this claim to all sentences of the form 'I don't know whether I am *present tense psychological verb* or not'. (Perhaps he would make this claim for many but not all verbs which name psychological states, processes, and so on.) And Section 246 suggests that he would claim that any sentence of the form, '[1] do(es) not know whether [2] is (am) *present tense psychological verb* or not', is meaningful if and only if the expressions inserted in slots 1 and 2 are used to refer to different persons. Here Wittgenstein is confusing the meaning (or meaningfulness) of a sentence with our fundamental beliefs about the state of affairs that is said to obtain by uttering the sentence.

Let us first note that neither Wittgenstein nor anyone else has offered any principle of language on which to base the claim that sentences of the form '[1] do(es) not know whether

The Significance of Sense

[2] is (am) *present tense psychological verb* or not' are not meaningful if the expressions put in 1 and 2 refer to the same person. The assertion that "doubt is logically excluded" (p. 221), whatever it may mean, is not a basis, since the purported meaninglessness of the sentence is supposed to explain, not be explained by, the purported logical exclusion of doubt. (Cf. Section 408.)

Secondly, maybe my imagination is defective, but the only way I can make the claim of meaninglessness sound remotely plausible is by attributing some ambiguity to that sentence-frame. How else could it be that sentences of that form are meaningless if and only if the referring expressions refer to the same person? But, as Fodor and Freed have pointed out, there just aren't any semantical or syntactical ambiguities to account for it.[8] What would the ambiguity be? Shall we suppose (as Wittgenstein may at one stage have done) that the psychological verbs like 'believe' and 'pain' (or rather, 'am in pain') are systematically ambiguous? But all the linguistic facts and principles are against such a supposition. First, this would be a clear violation of Putnam's rule. Furthermore, one will have a hard time explaining such facts as these: the assertion 'I am in pain.' is true if and only if the assertion 'He (or You) is (are) in pain.' (where 'I', 'He', and 'You' are being used to refer to the same person) is true; the uttering of the sentence 'I am in pain.' implies and counts as evidence for the truth of the assertion 'He is in pain.'; the utterance 'He said 'I am in pain.' is transformable into 'He said that he is in pain.'; the sentence 'I am in pain.' can be used to report what the sentence 'He is in pain.' can be used to state; and so on. Lastly, isn't it plainly perverse to suppose that the sentence 'I don't know whether Roger Wertheimer is in pain or not.' loses its sense whenever it emerges from *my* mouth—as

54

Counting Meanings

though I and I alone could suck all sense and life out of it?

But the clearest (though not the least controversial) proof that 'I don't know whether I am in pain or not.' is meaningful is that sometimes a statement made in uttering it (or similar expressions of doubt) is true. Some cases: (1) A doctor is probing around my injury and keeps asking if his probe hurts. I am certain that it does at the center of the injury and certain that it does not far outside the injured zone, but in the penumbra in between I am uncertain. (2) I have an injury and am engrossed in some activity (e.g., I am quarterbacking a Super Bowl game). Suddenly you ask me, 'Does your leg still hurt?'. My first reaction is to say, 'I don't know.', and then I may pause, direct my attention to my injury, and decide that it does—or that it does not—still hurt. (3) I have strained my back. You ask me if I am in pain. I reply, 'Well, I don't know. My back certainly aches, but is it a pain? Hmm, well, if I turn too quickly it hurts like hell, but am I really in pain at the moment? . . . I can't really say.' (4) You have malaria. All day you lie in bed moaning and screaming. Finally you fall asleep, but you keep on moaning, twisting and turning, sweating, and occasionally crying out. I check; you are definitely asleep. In the morning you feel better and I say to you, 'You were certainly in great pain last night.' You respond, 'Was I? I certainly didn't know it.'. (5) I am closely attentive to the state of my right arm and I say 'I don't know whether or not I have a severe pain or any pain at all in my right arm.'. Here my reader may find the case incomprehensible; he may say that he wouldn't know and can't imagine what that would be like. I would agree, however, such cases can and do exist. Due to an injury to some organ a person can know that he has a pain but be totally unable to locate it. (I have this on the authority of doctors and biologists.)

The Significance of Sense

Now suppose Ralph, an intelligent native speaker, is closely attending to the state of his whole body and sincerely says, 'I don't know whether or not I have a severe pain or any pain at all anywhere in my body.'.* Again my reader may say that this is incomprehensible, unimaginable, unintelligible, and inexplicable, and that it is odd for Ralph to say what he said in that situation. Again, I would agree. But the sentence he utters is not meaningless. It is not the sentence that is incomprehensible or unintelligible but the state of affairs said to obtain. It is odd for him to utter the sentence just because we fully understand what he is saying and *we cannot believe* that it is true—but it does not follow that it is not and cannot be true. What he says to be the case runs counter to all our experience, to our conception of our world, and so we cannot believe it, we cannot imagine it—but the limits of our imagination do not define the limits of the possible. We want to say that in that situation Ralph *can't help but know* whether or not he is in pain. Yet we already allow some failures to know (1–4) and are baffled by a new one (5), so why can't there be still others? We are assuming we already know every kind of failure to know whether oneself is in pain, but on what can we base that assumption? On a linguistic rule? Or on our system of beliefs as it now stands? We want to say that there *must* be some explanation of his failure to know. Yet we must grant that there is no set of nontrivial conditions (believing is a trivial condition) whose fulfillment logically necessitates that he knows. In the world as we now know it, such a case can't happen—but so what?

---

* Question: What makes him suppose that he *might* have a pain? Answer: Suppose he finds himself moaning, taking aspirin, putting ice packs on and holding his right arm. He has an urge to do these things, but he can't explain it even though he has a nasty bruise on his right arm.

Counting Meanings

Compare: Dwight is a sane, intelligent, native English speaker with normal human experience and perceptual capacities. He carefully observes a boy be hit by a car, have half his insides ripped out, drop at Dwight's feet, and give out heart-rending screams. Dwight then says, referring to the boy, 'I don't know whether he is in pain or not.'. Dwight will not be understood. What he says to be the case is wholly incomprehensible, unimaginable, inexplicable. The sentence he uttered has not thereby become meaningless. His audience understands his utterance, and just because they (we) do, they (we) are so baffled. What they cannot understand is Dwight—that is, *how* he could not know what he claims not to know. Here again, we want to say that there *must* be some explanation of his not knowing. But in my description of the case I have ruled out most and perhaps all of the usual explanations, and I can incorporate the denial of any further explanation you may offer. So as regards the possibility of failing to know, the cases of Ralph and Dwight are quite parallel.

I do not say that my knowing about my own pains is just like my knowing about your pains. Nor can I say how I know about your or my pains, and neither can I say why it is that, in fact, generally I can't help but know that I am in pain when I am. But one thing does seem clear: it is not my speaking English (or any other language) that makes me unable not to know.

Let us leave Wittgenstein and get back to the detection of ambiguities. There are various kinds and causes of ambiguity, and thus, various kinds of considerations and arguments that serve to locate and demonstrate an ambiguity. I am concerned only with the ambiguity of two words, 'right' and 'ought', and hence many kinds of considerations are irrelevant and many

57

forms of argument are unavailable. Since I am concerned with only those cases in which 'ought' is a modal auxiliary verb and 'right' is an adjective whose antonym is 'wrong', syntactical ambiguities are of no interest. Yet, syntactical considerations cannot be ignored, for what may look like a morphological ambiguity in 'right' or 'ought' may instead be a matter of syntax. Let us look at some other considerations.

Etymology can provide clues to word-ambiguity.[9] It does not with 'right' and 'ought' because, if these words have various senses, they bear to each other what I call an immediate natural relation. And when an ambiguity dispute concerns a word that is either univocal or has two immediately and naturally related senses, the etymological claims are question-begging. I shall try to explain this.

Let me clarify what I mean by "immediate natural relation" by contrasting it with other possibilities. I would say that some of the senses of 'bore' have an *accidental* relation to each other, because they derive from two different words in two different languages that happened to become phonetically and ideographically identical in our language. We might call these senses stepbrothers, for they are related only because their parents happened to marry. I would say that some of the senses of 'person' bear an *immediate artificial* relation to each other. The relation is immediate in that the two senses are quite similar. It is artificial in that one of the senses developed from the other by something like stipulation for the purposes of a specific activity. We might call these senses foster brothers, for one of them was legally adopted partly because of the nature of the natural child. I would say that some of the senses of 'bank' have a *distant natural* relation to each other, because, although both developed in nonartificial ways from the same

58

root, they are now distinct and disparate meanings without obvious similarities or interconnections. We might call these senses cousins.

Though my classification is neither well defined nor exhaustive, it should suffice to clarify what I mean by "immediate natural relation." Here the relationship would be that of either siblings or parent to child. The senses of the ambiguous phrase 'big boy' have an immediate natural relation. They are connected through the coincidence of developing size and maturity. If 'ought' or 'right' has various senses, it is a historical fact that they are naturally related, and it should be obvious that they are immediately related. (If it is not obvious now, it will become so later on.)

When senses are cousins, etymology is not needed to locate the senses; the glaring disparity renders the historical facts otiose. When senses are stepbrothers or foster brothers, etymology is helpful in ambiguity disputes because the artificiality of the relation is of some interest. But when the relation is a natural one, tracing the evolution of the word is a considerably more hazardous historical task. And if the relation is immediate as well, and someone doubts that there are two senses, the historical claims beg the question. It is no good arguing that only after such-and-such a date was the word used in a certain context or predicated of a certain kind of thing or something of this sort. Even if proved, it would not testify to a new sense, because, in effect, the issue is whether the "new use" is a use differing in a semantically relevant way. The change may be explicable without supposing a sense has evolved or emerged. This historical problem presupposes, and thus cannot provide, the solution to the semantic problem.

Take the following example. To a barbaric tribe the phrase 'a horrible worm' might be just as unintelligible as the phrase

The Significance of Sense

'an outrageous hexagon' is to us. They would never use the phrase and would not understand anybody who did. (I am supposing this to be determinable on fairly straightforward behavioristic grounds.) In brief, for them 'horrible' is impredicable of worms. (For that matter, we may as well suppose it to be impredicable of any small, harmless creature.) But as they become more civilized and more effete, the phrase might come to be intelligible to them and mean just the same to them as it does to us. This need not involve a change in the nature of worms or their knowledge of worms or the meaning of 'a' or 'horrible' or 'worm' or 'a horrible worm' or some other expression. Instead it may be simply (though it is not a simple phenomenon) that their attitudes toward worms and similar creatures have changed; they, the speakers themselves, have changed. In both their earlier and later cultures they might freely speak of someone being horrified by a worm, but only in their earlier culture would they think such a man mad or possessed. Just so, we might speak of someone being outraged by a hexagon and think him paranoid schizophrenic. Yet only at their "advanced" stage would they say that a worm can actually be horrible, just as we do not speak of hexagons as actually being outrageous.* Thus, even if 'right' or 'ought' lacked a certain use until, say, the twentieth century, that by itself shows nothing about a new or different sense of the word.

Extensional considerations are also of little value in regard to the ambiguity of 'ought' and 'right'. The extension of a word is the class of all and only those objects of which the word

* The issues raised by such cases are various and important. They bear on the nature of analytic and necessary truths, on the nature of category mistakes, and on the relation of language to the speakers of the language. This case could also be profitably related to the problem of the meaningfulness of 'I don't know whether I am in pain or not.'.

can be truly predicated. But since 'ought' is a modal auxiliary verb, not a predicate, it has no extension. So one would have to consider the extension of the expression 'ought to VP' for each verb phrase, and see if something is common to all and only those members of the extension of 'ought to VP' for each verb phrase. However, that would be fruitless. In general, for any object x which is a member of the extension of 'ought to VP_1' one can find another verb phrase such that x is also a member of the extension of 'ought to VP_2'.

Much the same applies to 'right'. Though 'right' is an adjective, it need not be a predicate. Its surface grammar suggests that at least some of the time it is syncategorematic. (I.e., it marks out a category of objects not on its own, but only with (*syn*) another term that does.[10]) When 'right' appears in sentences of the form 'NP_1 (noun phrase) is (not) the right NP_2', we cannot speak of the extension of 'right' per se, but only of the extension of 'right NP' for each noun phrase. Yet, for any object x which is a member of the extension of 'right NP_2' one can find another noun phrase such that x is also a member of the extension of 'right NP_3'. So even if extensional considerations are relevant, their application would require some other kinds of considerations.

Sommers has suggested the following test for heterotypical ambiguity:

If a, b, and c are any three things and P and Q are predicates such that it makes sense to predicate P of a and b but not of c and it makes sense to predicate Q of b and c but not of a, then P must be equivocal over a and b or Q must be equivocal over b and c. Conversely, if P and Q are univocal predicates, then there can be no three things a, b, c such that P applies to a and b but not to c while Q applies to b and c but not to a.[11]

The Significance of Sense

While agreeing with Sommers that heterotypical predication need not involve ambiguity, I find his arguments and his rule without merit.* His article opens with an attack on the alleged heterotypical ambiguity of 'exist'. Though he never applies his rule to 'exist' his claim that 'exist' is univocal is in conformity with his rule—trivially so. According to that rule, any word (i.e., predicate) predicable into every type is univocal. Thus 'exists' is univocal just because there is no thing c such that it makes no sense to predicate 'exist' of c, while there is some term Q which is predicable of c. So too, if 'right' and 'ought' are treated as predicates, they would be shown to be univocal just because they are predicable into every type. Surely, an ambiguist would be undissuaded by being told that they are univocal because they are predicable of every kind of thing. After all, if we drop the restriction that its antonym be 'wrong', the adjective 'right' abounds in disparate senses.

---

* For example, he claims (contra Quine) that 'hard' is ambiguous over chairs and questions. The only reason he gives independent of his rule is that if 'hard' were univocal, "then we could perfectly well say that this question is harder than that chair." He gives no hint as to why it follows that we could perfectly well say that. It does not follow at all. 'Hard' is not ambiguous over chairs and surfaces but it is odd to say that this surface is harder than that chair. It is odd to say that this hat is better than that table, but not only is 'good' univocal over hats and tables, hats and tables are of the same type. Of course, a perfectly good sense can be given to any of these comparative assertions: this question is harder relative to other questions than that chair is hard relative to other chairs.

The heterotypical ambiguity of 'hard' is shown by its having the antonym 'soft' when applied to 'chairs' and 'easy' when applied to questions. When its antonym is 'easy' it can appear in the environment 'NP is hard to VP' but not 'NP is hard to the NP'. Just the opposite obtains when its antonym is 'soft'. Compare: 'That lump is hard to touch.', "That lump is hard to the touch.'.

62

Counting Meanings

A more serious kind of consideration is that of paraphrasability. Suppose that the set of utterances in which a word w can appear is divisible into two subsets A and B such that in an A utterance w is replaceable by the expression x but not by the expression y without changing the meaning of the utterance, while in B utterances y can but x cannot replace w without changing the meaning of the utterance.* This might seem sufficient grounds for calling w ambiguous over A and B utterances.

This criterion fails since it tests utterances, not sentences, thereby overlooking factors other than the meaning(s) of w. Suppose I say 'I shall do it.' and you ask 'What do you mean?'. I may reply, 'I mean I intend to do it.'. Or suppose I say 'We'll smoke some tea.', and you ask, 'What do you mean 'we'?', and I reply, 'I mean all the guys in the frat.'. In both cases my reply gives what I mean, not what the words mean. Two expressions may be used to express what the speaker means without themselves meaning the same.

Yet even if we tested sentences instead of utterances, we would not get a sufficient condition of word ambiguity, for the differences in paraphrasability may still be due to factors other than the meaning(s) of w. Take the relative adjective 'expensive'. Any sentence of the form 'NP_1 is an expensive NP_2' is paraphrasable by a correlative sentence of the form 'NP_1 is a more expensive NP_2 than the average (or normal or standard) NP_2'. Identifying the meaning of 'expensive' with the expression substituted for it, 'more expensive NP_2 than the average', would compel us to say that 'expensive' is ambiguous, for that expression is not substitutable for the appearance of 'expensive' inside itself. The result of that substitution is the absurdity:

---

* There might also be a subset C in which w is replaceable by both x and y.

'NP_1 is a more more expensive NP_2 than the average NP_2 than the average NP_2'. Since this difficulty arises with almost any relative adjective ('tiny', 'fast'), Putnam's rule demands the rejection of this criterion of ambiguity.*

The difficulty stems from the paraphrase's being a paraphrase of a syntactical structure, not of a specific word in the sentence. But even after avoiding that difficulty, one might still be paraphrasing a sentence, not just a word, in that the information (not the meanings per se) carried by the rest of the sentence may suggest one rather than another paraphrase of the word. (Compare: A turquoise object will be described as greenish-blue or bluish-green depending on its environment.) Sometimes 'fortunate' is paraphrasable by 'lucky', sometimes not. If I say, 'I was fortunate to be elected President.' I might resist the paraphrase 'lucky' because of its implication that it was due to luck that I was elected. In other cases the implication would be harmless. This points to a further problem: what is to count as a paraphrase?

If a paraphrase must be a synonym, then to show a paraphrasability difference would be to show that a word is synonymous with two nonsynonymous expressions—and that virtually entails that a word is ambiguous.† A univocalist is

---

* The point here should not be confused with another feature of relative adjectives, that of having both a syncategorematic and a quasi-attributive use. Compare: 'The Atlantic is a big ocean.', 'The Atlantic is big.'. The former is false, the latter true. In the first the class of comparison is specified: 'ocean', but the second is used with a vague and unspecified (and perhaps unspecifiable) class of comparison. It is not that the Atlantic is a big something-or-other; it is just big. Yet I see no reason to assign a morphological ambiguity here.

† I say 'virtually' because I will contend that 'can' is univocal even though it is sometimes synonymous with 'may' and sometimes (almost) synonymous with 'is able', yet 'may' and 'is able' are quite different in meaning.

not likely to concede that both of the paraphrases are true synonyms. But if an adequate paraphrase need only be very similar (not the same) in meaning to the word, then paraphrasability seems too weak for a criterion of word ambiguity because a univocal word may be like each of two paraphrases which are unlike each other (i.e., the meaning of w is, in one respect, like the meaning of x and, in a different respect, like that of y.) * In short, paraphrasability seems either too good a criterion or not good enough.

Nonetheless, differences in paraphrase are worth noting. When the ambiguity of w is disputed and both parties admit that there are paraphrasability differences in connection with w, then the burden of proof should be on the univocalist to show that the differences are explicable without supposing w to be ambiguous. (This is one of the tasks of an adequate univocalist account of 'right' and 'ought'.) It should not be incumbent upon the ambiguist to prove that only an ambiguity could explain the paraphrasability difference. (Of course, the univocalist may deny that there are such differences; he may reject all or some of the purported paraphrases as inadequate. The argument may then come to a halt from lack of shared linguistic intuitions.) But contrariwise, the greater the number of expressions paraphrasing w throughout a class of utterances, the more likely it is that w is univocal over that class (Putnam's rule). This is extendable by including what I call companion expressions, that is, synonyms, near synonyms, antonyms, and near antonyms of w, as well as other expressions having some semantic relation to w. Then it can be said that the greater the number of expressions maintaining their companion relation to w throughout a class of utterances in which w appears,

---

* This would serve to explain how 'true' sometimes is and sometimes is not a paraphrase of 'right'.

The Significance of Sense

the more likely it is that w is univocal over that class. If the class is the class of all utterances in which w can appear, this principle is a test of word univocity.

This principle lies at the heart of my account of 'ought'. Thus, it is important that 'should' can always replace 'ought'. Ambiguists might take this as showing only that 'should' is ambiguous in the same ways as 'ought'. But that move becomes less attractive as more companion words are seen to maintain their relation to 'ought' throughout all the utterances in which 'ought' appears. The principle is less directly applicable to 'right'. Since I have demarcated the relevant uses of 'right' by its antonymous relation with 'wrong', I cannot use that relation as evidence for the univocity of 'right'. (Nonetheless, it is striking that 'wrong' maintains that relation throughout a class of utterances over which 'right' is thought to be ambiguous.) Furthermore, no single paraphrase of 'right' (or 'wrong') is common to the whole class of utterances. The etymologically related word 'correct' comes close, but even it is out of place in many contexts. Such facts require explanation.

The relation of word ambiguity to sentence ambiguity may seem to offer a test of word ambiguity. But being a potential source of sentence ambiguity is not even a necessary condition of word ambiguity since sometimes the two senses of a word are connected to different syntactical features, thereby preventing the two senses from coexisting in any appearance of the word (e.g., 'grande' in Spanish).* Barring such syntactical interference, being a potential source of sentence ambiguity may well be a necessary condition of word ambiguity. Yet this cannot be so glibly used as a sufficient condition of word

---

* This could not happen with 'ought', but if 'right' is ambiguous, its ambiguity might be of this sort.

ambiguity. What is to count as a *source* of sentence ambiguity? Take the syntactically ambiguous sentence 'Failing freshmen delighted me.'. Replacing 'delighted' by 'delights' cancels one interpretation; replacing it instead by 'hanged' cancels the other interpretation. Replacing 'freshmen' by 'algebra' cancels both interpretations (i.e., it forces a different use of 'failing'). Is 'delighted' or '-ed' a *source* of sentence ambiguity here? Is 'freshmen'? Neither 'delighted' nor '-ed' nor 'freshmen' is ambiguous—and even if they are, that has nothing to do with the ambiguity of the sentence.* So I don't see how to formulate a sufficient condition of word ambiguity in terms of sentence ambiguity. (N.B.: I don't claim it can't be done.)

Moreover, it is no easier to establish the ambiguity of a sentence than of a word. Intuitively, if 'We ought to be there soon.' is ambiguous, then 'ought' is the source of the ambiguity. But is the sentence ambiguous? Multiple illocutionary potential and multiple propositional potential provide the most tempting criteria of sentence ambiguity,† because the properties of illocutions and propositions allow them to be counted in ways that sentence meanings cannot. Declarative illocutions and propositions have truth values while sentences and their meanings do not, so one might count sets of associable truth conditions to determine the number of sentence meanings. Nondeclarative illocutions have other features which could be used in a similar way (e.g., different promises are fulfilled by different actions). Furthermore, on independent grounds, it has often been thought that sentence meaning *is* the illocutionary or propositional potential of a sentence. Alston ex-

---

* It seems that 'right' in 'It is right that he is the owner.' is like 'delighted' in 'Failing freshmen delighted me.'; these words allow certain syntactical ambiguities to be realized.

† According to such criteria 'We ought to be there soon.' is ambiguous.

plicitly identifies the meaning of a sentence with its illocutionary act potential.[12] In a similar vein Fodor and Freed suggest that a sentence is ambiguous if and only if it has two or more sets of associated conditions (i.e., states of affairs associated with the utterance of the sentence in standard cases).[13] And as Searle's work makes evident, the pre-Austinian talk of propositions and propositional contents provides additional variants of this theme.[14] However, there are problems about all this, but before investigating them I must pause to establish some terminology and remove some potential red herrings.

I do not wish to talk as Ziff does when he says that "a sentence-token is ambiguous if and only if in employing the token one is making an ambiguous remark, or comment, statement, observation, etc.".[15] I prefer to talk in a way indicated by Austin's terminology such that an illocution (a remark, comment, statement, observation) or a proposition cannot be ambiguous. The performance of an illocutionary speech act and the correlative illocution presuppose the performance of an act of using a particular pheme (sentence) * with a certain more or less definite sense and a more or less definite reference.[16] Thus, when I say 'Capote threw the ball.', the sentence (pheme) that I utter is ambiguous, but the proposition and the illocution that I produce are not, for I mean by 'Capote' a particular man, by 'ball' a gala party, and so on. To be sure, one may misunderstand me and think that I meant by 'ball' a spheroid object. This shows, not that my illocution is ambiguous, but that it may be unclear *what* illocution I am producing.† So, let me reformulate Ziff's criterion: a sentence

---

* We can take what Austin means by 'pheme' to be what I mean by 'sentence'.

† If the position I am taking were to be systematically worked out, allowance would have to be made for cases such as puns and double entendres. These cases are irrelevant to my purposes and I am not aiming for comprehensiveness, so I shall ignore these details.

is ambiguous if and only if there could be some occasion on which its utterance is reasonably construable by an intelligent native speaker as being either of two or more illocutions.

Note that I am taking sentence ambiguity to be a function of the syntactical and morphological structure of a sentence,[17] not, as some writers have done,[18] of the likelihood that an audience will perceive more than one possible interpretation. Thus, each sentence-token possesses every ambiguity of its sentence-type. Granted, given the context of utterance and the assumption that the speaker is speaking rationally, coherently, and relevantly, the audience can often ignore all but one of the possible interpretations. (E.g., While you are fumbling at the lock I say to you 'You are using the wrong key.'.) The other interpretations are, in such a context, dead possibilities, not because the sentence-token *cannot* be meant or understood in those ways, but because those interpretations are inappropriate and thus not likely to be meant by the speaker. If the speaker means the sentence-token in one of its dead intepretations, his behavior is bizarre, but the sense of what he says (the sentence) is not impugned. (I could have meant that you are using the wrong musical key—even if I know that you do not play an instrument.) Thus, the sole point of bringing in speech contexts at all is that it enables me to talk about illocutions.

Again, the proposed criterion is that a sentence is ambiguous if and only if there could be some occasion on which its utterance is reasonably construable by an intelligent native speaker as being either of two or more illocutions. This criterion will not do. First, it is not a sufficient condition. As Austin rightly notes, many uncertainties about the kind of illocution being made are independent of the meaning of the sentence uttered.[19] If someone says 'Come here.' we may wonder whether he is ordering, requesting, or inviting, and if he says 'I'll do it.' we may wonder whether he is promising or only expressing an intention. If the criterion is altered so that the two construed illocutions must be of the same kind (e.g., both are orders or both are statements), it ceases to be a necessary condition of sentence ambiguity. The interpretations of some ambiguous sentences are associable with quite different kinds of illocutions: 'You stay here when I leave.', 'I promise to exercise every day.', 'Let us pray.'.*

These last cases suggest another revised criterion: a sentence is ambiguous if and only if it is associable with two quite different kinds of illocutions (e.g., a declarative illocution and a promise). Certainly this has no chance as a necessary condition of sentence ambiguity, but neither is it a sufficient condition. Recall that sentences of the form: 'I shall VP, or 'I *present tense verb/future indicating adverb*' † ('I leave tomorrow.') are associable with predictions and expressions of intention. Call these FF sentences (for first person future). Another class of counterexamples consists of sentences of the form, '*proper name/third person present tense illocutionary verb/object of verb*'.‡ Call these PI sentences (for proper name illocutionary verb). A PI sentence like 'The United States promises to defend South Vietnam.' is associable with both declarative illocutions and promises, but that is no reason to think such a sentence ambiguous. What would be the source of the ambiguity? If it were a morphological ambiguity it would have to lie in the illocutionary verb, so are we to suppose that 'promise' has a descriptive and a promissive

---

* Note that if one were to talk as Ziff does one would be hard put to say *what* kind of illocution is ambiguous in such cases.

† The specification here is rather crude; it gives neither a necessary nor a sufficient condition for belonging to the class I have in mind.

‡ Again, the specification is not strictly correct since some illocutionary verbs (e.g., 'insult') are not normally used when producing the illocution named by the verb.

meaning, that 'apologize' has a descriptive and an apologetic meaning, that 'congratulate' has a descriptive and a congratulatory meaning, and so on?

However, this only shows that no morphological ambiguity explains the multiple illocutionary potential of PI sentences. Someone might think that PI sentences are syntactically ambiguous, but such a person would probably be confusing three different uses of a sentence like, 'The United States promises to negotiate every day.'.

A. A promise (said by, e.g., an ambassador): The U.S. will negotiate every day.
B. A declarative illocution:
  1. There is something the U.S. promises, namely to negotiate every day.
  2. There is something the U.S. does every day, namely promise to negotiate.

The difference between A and B1 involves no ambiguity, but B2 is a possible reading due to a syntactical ambiguity connected with the habitual aspect of the verb. (FF sentences like 'I leave when the time comes.' are susceptible to a similar treatment.)

The relations between the potential illocutions of FF and PI sentences do not require an ambiguity; on the contrary, they require that the sentence be used in the same sense. As was noted with FF sentences like 'I shall sing.', saying it gives good grounds for believing it—and that is the *point* of saying it. With PI sentences like 'The United States promises to defend South Vietnam.', the speaker intends to be making a promise in virtue of which subsequent utterances of the same sentence are true declarative illocutions. Saying it makes it so—and that is the *point* of saying it.

And now it should be obvious that FF and PI sentences are not alone in having multiple illocutionary potential without being ambiguous. For a vast array of sentences, their initial issuance (from the mouths of legislators or the like) is a rule, law, definition, directive, prohibition, permission, or the like, which has consequences for subsequent issuances of the same sentence. If Congress says 'Income tax returns must be filed by April 15.' it is enacting a law (something lacking a truth-value) in virtue of which subsequent utterances of the same sentence are true declarative illocutions. If instead Congress says 'Income tax returns will be filed by April 15.' it does not follow that income tax returns *actually* will be filed by April 15. Congress's utterance is *some* evidence that subsequent utterances will be true, but, more important, it constitutes a reason for making it true. That is, subsequent utterances will be true if everyone does as the law directs; if someone does not file by April 15, he is doing something wrong (violating a law). I shall return to this point in the next chapter.

We have just seen that a sentence's being associable with two different kinds of illocutions is neither necessary nor sufficient for the sentence's being ambiguous. So let us amend the criterion: a sentence is ambiguous if and only if its utterance on some occasion is reasonably construable as being either of two (or more) illocutions which differ not merely (if at all) in being two different kinds of illocutions. That is, if and only if the difference between the two illocutions is more than just a difference in the kinds of illocution (e.g., promise and statement), the sentence is ambiguous. This seems to be a necessary condition of sentence ambiguity, but it is certainly not a sufficient condition, because different statements (or other kinds of declarative illocutions) having different truth-conditions and truth-values can be produced with the same univocal sentence. That is, some univocal sentences have multiple propositional potential. There are at least five kinds of cases of this. (The fifth is presented in the next chapter.)

First, multiple propositional potential may be due to referential variability. The sentence, 'He is a vegetarian.' is not ambiguous, yet in uttering it I might be referring to Ted or Ned but not both. Thus, I could be forming the proposition that Ted is a vegetarian or that Ned is a vegetarian, and these propositions have different truth-conditions and may differ in truth-value.

Second, the appearance of syncategorematic words can be a source of multiple propositional potential unconnected with sentence ambiguity. The unambiguous sentence, 'Tige is tiny.' may be used to make various statements depending on whether what is meant by the speaker is that Tige is tiny for a Pomeranian, tiny for a dog, tiny for a mammal, or so on. Again, these different statements have different truth-conditions and may differ in truth-value.

Third, those PI sentences whose illocutionary verb names a declarative illocution are associable with two illocutions of that kind and two propositions. A sentence like 'The United States asserts that its ships never entered North Korean waters.' is not ambiguous, but two different assertions could be made in uttering it. One could be asserting either that the United States ships never entered North Korean waters or that the United States asserts that its ships never entered North Korean waters. What gets asserted in these two cases has different truth-conditions and may have differing truth values.*

---

* Truth and falsity are predicated of propositions, assertions, statements, and similar declarative illocutions, and since usually what is said (in one sense of 'what is said') is a declarative illocution, it can be called

The Significance of Sense

Fourth, the appearance of what unfortunately has been called a parenthetical verb,[20] may enable an unambiguous sentence to have multiple propositional potential. Sentences like 'I believe he is here.' may be either a report on one's beliefs or a guarded report on the thing believed. These reports have different truth-conditions and may differ in truth-value.* But there is no reason to think that 'believe', 'suspect', 'regret', and the rest of the parenthetical verbs are ambiguous, or that sentences in which they appear are, for that very reason, ambiguous.

Let me draw some morals from my discussion of sentence ambiguity. The relation of sentence meaning to truth-conditions appears looser and more complex than is often thought. The peculiar properties of the sentences I have discussed (especially the FF, PI, and parenthetical verb sentences) seem to be a function of the special relation a speaker has to his own words. Such sentences have no exotic semantic features: performative verbs are simply names of actions performable by uttering words; parenthetical verbs are names of certain propositional attitudes and actions; FF sentences can use any verb phrase in-

---

true or false. But when what is asserted is that the U.S. ships never entered North Korean waters, what is asserted is not what is said (i.e., 'The U.S. asserts that . . . .'), so what is said has no truth-value, but what is asserted does.

* Urmson thinks that utterances of the form 'I believe that p' (or 'I regret that p', etc.) cannot be reports on a "psychological condition," true if and only if the speaker believes (regrets, etc.) p. But note the following dialogue: 'Who among you believes that Jones is now in Buffalo?'—'I believe that Jones is now in Buffalo.'. Of course, in both the parenthetical and nonparenthetical uses, if what is believed is not the case, then the audience may say 'You are mistaken.', but it does not follow from this that, in the nonparenthetical use, what is said is false. (Cf. pp. 29–30 on 'intend' and 'shall'.) I suspect that it is due to this mistake that Urmson treats the parenthetical use as primary and the nonparenthetical as derivative. Surely, just the opposite is true.

dicating futurity and predicable of a speaker. (The first two classes intersect and are each subsets of the third.) And their syntactical structure is unaltered by a noun phrase not referring to the speaker. I suspect that the problems surrounding the relation of a speaker to his words are quite perplexing; not surprisingly they have gone undiscussed, indeed, virtually unmentioned. Though not itself a meaning or semantic relation, it is the nexus of the relation of language to human rationality and action. It is, I think, the key to the various aspects of the egocentric predicament—psychological, epistemological, and moral. But that is merely an educated guess.

PI sentences can teach another lesson, one that has been taught before: the fact that a specific word is the source of a sentence's being associable with a special kind of illocution does not show that the word has a special *kind* of meaning.[21] If 'brave' is inserted into the sentence-environment 'You are _____' then the sentence is associable with praise and commendation. If 'degenerate' is put in the same slot, the sentence is associable with criticism and condemnation. It does not follow that 'brave' and 'degenerate' have an evaluative or emotive meaning lacked by 'right-handed'. The relationship between the words and the illocutions is completely explicable in terms of *our* normal *beliefs* and *attitudes* toward brave men, degenerates, and right-handers. To import such matters into the meanings of words is, in general, not only otiose, but disastrous for a proper understanding of language and human rationality.

Except for a relatively small number of words like 'hello', a word can be used in an unlimited number of sentence-environments. Only a small percentage of the sentences thus formed have a strong relation to some particular illocution. Yet, independently of their relation to particular illocutions, these sentences are connected to each other through a net of semantic and syntactic relations—but the sentences could not be so interconnected if the meanings of the words shifted according to the illocutions with which the sentences are associable. My point is really a truism: words and sentences do not evaluate, prescribe, describe, or emote—only a speaker can do such things. The fact that we do certain of these things more with some words than others is in part a consequence of the meaning of the words—but only in part. It is as much a consequence of our beliefs and attitudes about the things in our world. Some of those beliefs and attitudes are as deep in us as they are common, and some of them are virtually universal.*

---

* In a recent article, Hare tries to avoid the consequences of these and other points I have discussed about word meaning and illocutions. The claim that seems to get the whole argument of that article in motion is that "there are some expressions whose meaning has to be explained in terms of speech acts." [22] Hare defends this claim by adducing the word 'promise' as an example. I confess to being genuinely boggled by this, because the example trivializes the claim. Of course the meaning of 'promise' has to be explained in terms of speech acts; it is the *name* of one! So too, there are some expressions whose meaning has to be explained in terms of snipes, e.g., 'dowitcher'. Once it is appreciated that 'promise', like 'snivel', is the name of an action, both the elaborate syntactical machinery and the analogy with 'good' which he produces seem far-fetched. And Hare does not provide a reason for denying that 'promise' is simply the name of an action, for there is none. *Perhaps* he is misled by the fact that, when to say 'NP promise that p' is to promise, one does not *assert* that NP promises that p, but rather *makes* the promise. If this is the cause of confusion, then perhaps it is worth remembering that, though one does not assert it, one does *tell* one's audience that NP promises that p, and in virtue of telling it, it is true. This comes across even more clearly with utterances such as, 'I'm warning you for the last time to stay away from my daughter.'.

Three

The Meanings of the Modals

> Within the modal system English does not distinguish
> between duty and logic. And if not there, English can't
> do it anywhere within the whole grammatical system.
> —Martin Joos, *The English Verb*

IT is useful and perhaps necessary to nest an account of 'ought'
inside a general account of the modal auxiliary verbs. And if an
account of the modals is to be useful, it is necessary to deal
with various issues, some of which are complex and some
philosophical. Since I wish my account to be untendentious,
I try to pare down my philosophical commitments to a minimum. But the complexities are unavoidable; I hope my reader
will bear with them.

'Ought' is synonymous with 'should' when 'should' is not a
past or conditional form of 'shall'. (Hereafter, the 'should'
synonymous with 'ought' is written 'shought'.) I write about
'ought' because it is simpler, since 'should' is ambiguous and
'ought' is not. The ambiguity of 'should' is the source of the
ambiguity of:

(1)   I should like to thank you.

The Significance of Sense

The very fact that 'ought' and 'shought' belong to the select grammatical class of modal auxiliary verbs and share the same range of uses is a reason for claiming that both are univocal over that range. And it is further evidence of this that though they derive from different words, both were originally the preterite form of verbs meaning 'to owe'. (See pp. 130–132.)

Other similarities and differences deserve mention. The use of 'ought' has been more stable than that of 'should'. The meaning of 'ought' traces back at least to the Elizabethan era, the major modification being the gradual extinction of the alternative senses.* Yet, something like a dim recognition of its original form as a preterite verb seems to persist in the now substandard phrase 'hadn't ought to', and the more acceptable tag-questions using 'had':

(2)   We ought to leave now, hadn't we?

This is not to be found with 'shought'. The only recent notable change in 'ought' I have unearthed is the emergence within the last century of the mandatory insertion of 'to' between 'ought' and the verb.† Since 'shought' does not take this 'to', it is natural that its usage diverge somewhat from that of 'ought'. Compare:

(3)   Why should the man be punished?
(4)   Why ought the man to be punished? (Or perhaps: Why ought the man be punished?)

---

* But see note, p. 120 for a possible counterindication.

† Some linguists contend that the 'to' indicates that 'ought' is not a genuine modal auxiliary. But since, in every other respect, 'ought' is just like the rest of the modals, I see no basis for that claim. Besides, it is hard to say just how mandatory the 'to' is. It is regularly deleted in interrogatives. Even in indicatives the situation is unclear. Often it is pronounced 'oughta' as though it were a single word. Moreover, though 'You ought not go.' is somewhat improper, it sounds no worse than 'Just between you and I . . .' which is commonly said.

The Meanings of the Modals

The mandatory 'to' often makes the use of 'ought' awkward. In particular, 'shought' is preferred where an interpolation between 'ought' and 'to' would be required, as in questions. (Frequently the 'to' is dropped in questions, but perhaps just because of that, 'ought' is still awkward.) Thus, in general 'ought' tends to require a more careful style of speech than 'shought', and this in turn may explain the fact that 'shought' is more commonly used, and the related fact that 'ought' sounds more formal and more emphatic.

In at least two contexts 'shought' is permitted and 'ought' excluded on something other than stylistic ground. First, where the auxiliary verb is operating in the real past:

(5)   When Alexi entered the theater, whom should he meet but Arnold!

(6)   When Alexi entered the theater, whom ought he to meet but Arnold!

6 is odd, 5 is not. This use of 'shought' is restricted to expressions of surprise, indignation, irony and the like. ('Must' has a similar use.) The second context is that in which a subjunctive equivalent is employed.

(7)   It is high time we should rid ourselves of such scoundrels.

(8)   It is high time we ought to rid ourselves of such scoundrels.

Such differences as these and the one concerning tag-questions may be freaks of idiom and not revelatory of significant semantical or syntactical differences.*

Ziff attempts to distinguish 'ought' from 'should',[1] but since,

---

* Much of the foregoing is based on the work of Ehrman and Jespersen. John Cooper set me straight about 7.

apparently, he assumes that 'should' is univocal, he fails.* The crucial step in his argument is that 9 is deviant and 10 is not.

(9)   I ought to do it if I were you.
(10)   I should do it if I were you.

But the 'should' of 10 is the conditional form of 'shall'; it is not 'shought'. Take a parallel example in which 'should' cannot be the conditional form of 'shall'.

(11)   If he had told you, it should have set your mind at ease.
(12)   If he had told you, it ought to have set your mind at ease.
(13)   If he had told you, it would have set your mind at ease.

Only 13 with its conditional form, 'would', is nondeviant. 'Ought' and 'shought' are in the same boat; they are not used as conditional forms and hence cannot appear in the consequent of a contrary-to-fact conditional. But for that matter, neither can 'shall', 'will', 'can', 'may', or 'must'. However, these other modals have corresponding expressions which do the job: 'shall' has 'should', 'will' has 'would', 'can' has 'could', 'may' has 'might', and 'must' has 'had to'. (This last is special since 'had to' is not a modal auxiliary.) 'Ought' and 'shought' lack correlative conditional forms, but I doubt that this indicates anything of interest. After all, what is said with a contrary-to-fact conditional is expressible by other means. Anyway, if this lacuna has a rationale, it may well be compatible with my account of 'ought'.

---

* Ultimately I think it must be conceded that 'shought' is not a *perfect* synonym of 'ought'. The differences are more easily described once the framework of my account is at hand. See note, p. 98.

The Meanings of the Modals

In my account, instead of defining 'ought' directly, a formal definition is given of the sentence-frame 'n ought to v' where 'n' is some noun phrase and 'v' is some verb phrase. The word 'ought' places no restrictions on the contents of 'n' and 'v' except for those common to modal auxiliaries in general * (e.g., the main verb of 'v' takes its infinitival form). If the correlative sentence 'n v' (where the main verb of 'v' takes a finite form) is a grammatical sentence, then 'n ought to v' is a grammatical sentence. Of course, a proposition 'n ought to v' may be false, even wildly false, while the correlative proposition 'n v' is true, but that is a different matter. Thus one requirement of an adequate univocalist account of 'ought' is that it place no restrictions on the possible contents of 'n' and 'v'. My account meets this condition.

I reach the definition of 'ought' by locating its relations to and differences from 'must', 'can', and 'is' (or 'shall' or 'will'). More precisely, the primary data concern the logical relations of the sentence-frame 'n ought to v' to the correlative sentence-frames 'n must v', 'n can v', and 'n v'.† My strategy here is recommended by two considerations. First, these matters have to be discussed eventually, for without them my account would be devoid of philosophical interest. Secondly, intuitively it seems significant that 'ought' and its sole synonym are members of the small and special class of modal auxiliary verbs. A cursory investigation suggests that the modals form something of a semantic system; a careful in-

---

* Some instructive exceptions to this principle will be dealt with as we proceed.

† 'n v' does duty for the present and future of 'v'. Thus, the sentence correlative to 'I ought to go.' may be either 'I go.', 'I am going.', or 'I shall (will) go.'. This variability of 'n v' is required by the fact that 'n ought to v' can have present or future reference. That is, 'I ought to go.' may be said of my present act of going or of some future act of going.

vestigation shows that the place of 'ought' in this system is virtually definitive of 'ought'.

Before these latter points can be made evident we must divest ourselves of some linguistic prejudices. First, we have to abandon the dogma of the defenders of "proper speech" that 'can' is never interchangeable with 'may'. Most descriptive linguists view this as being outdated normative nonsense. 'Can' is freely substitutable for 'may' where 'may' is so used that 'n may v and n may not v' is a contradiction.*

We must also free ourselves of the more insidious preconceptions about 'ought' that have developed within our philosophical tradition. My account may be rejected out of hand by philosophers whose ears have been so blunted by that tradition that they are incapable of distinguishing 'ought' from 'must' (or the synonyms of 'must': 'have to', 'have got to', and 'got to').† Philosophers have assumed that, at least in moral contexts, 'n ought to v' means or implies that n's doing v is in conformity with some law. But this is actually a crude definition of 'n must v'—or at least leaves no room for a distinction between 'ought' and 'must'. I shall devote a good deal of space to that distinction, but for the moment let us merely glance at the following rack of cases. In each pair the even-numbered utterance sounds odd (16 sounds positively ungrammatical) and the odd-numbered utterance does not.

(14)   Your brother's life is at stake and he has no one else to turn to now. You ought to help him.

---

* In the terminology I shall develop, this point is expressed by saying that, where the relevant System is an Ideal System, 'n can v' is equivalent to 'n may v'.

† That philosophers confuse 'ought' and 'must' was first pointed out to me by Stanley Cavell.

(15) Your brother's life is at stake and he has no one else to turn to now. You must help him.

(16) You ought, you absolutely ought to tell her what you have done. You have no right and no excuse not to tell her.

(17) You must, you absolutely must tell her what you have done. You have no right and no excuse not to tell her.

(18) If you don't want to go nuts in this business, you simply ought to get yourself a decent secretary.

(19) If you don't want to go nuts in this business, you simply must get yourself a decent secretary.

In all cases 'must' sounds considerably stronger than 'ought'. I shall contend that 'n must v' always entails and is never entailed by 'n ought to v'.*

The modal auxiliary system contains twelve words, but, for my purposes, less than half need attention. Four of them, 'could', 'might', 'would', and 'should' (not 'shought'), are essentially past or conditional forms of four other modals: 'can', 'may', 'will', and 'shall'. The modal use of two words, 'dare' and 'need', is dying out, especially in America. The main modal use of 'need' is in 'n need not v' which serves as a sentential negation of 'n must v'. (Other sentential negations of 'n must v' are 'n does not have to v' and 'n has not got to v', but neither of these are modals.) Finally, though 'shall' and 'will' are not strictly synonymous, they may be equated since the primary use of both is as something like future tense forms of the copula.

This hasty inspection leaves five words: 'will' (or 'shall'),

---

* This presupposes what I take to be a truism: What is entailed by a proper assertion may not be properly assertible.

'must', 'ought' (or 'shought'), 'may', and 'can'. Intuitively, 'must' expresses the idea of necessity, 'can' that of possibility, and 'will' that of future actuality. These seem linked in that what is necessary is (or will be) actual, and what is actual is possible, and what is not possible is necessarily not actual, and what is not necessary is possible. Further, while 'may' is sometimes interchangeable with 'can', in another set of uses 'may' means something stronger than 'can'. To say 'He may succeed.' is to say more than that it is possible he will succeed; it implies that there is some probability (unspecified— it can be high or low) that he will succeed.* 'Ought' fits between 'must' and 'may' (or 'might'); it is weaker than 'must' and stronger than 'may', even where 'may' is stronger than 'can'. To say 'The roast ought to be done.' is to say more than that there is some probability that it is done; it implies that the probability is fairly high or that one can legitimately expect it to be done. Such facts suggest that the definition of 'ought' may be a precipitate of an examination of the other modals and their relation to 'ought'. It turns out that a definition of 'may' is not essential for this, and that 'shall' and 'will' are best treated as forms of the copula, and thus that only 'must' and 'can' need to be defined.

My account of the modals (i.e., 'must', 'can', and 'ought') is shaped by two requirements of any adequate definition: the definition must not be (viciously) circular, and the definiens must have all and only those logical relations possessed by the definiendum. Both conditions pose special problems for

---

* Our estimate of the probability derives from our beliefs concerning the state of affairs, n v. Naturally the speech context must also be taken into account. A similar point applies where 'can' *seems* to express a probability. (See p. 99.)

definitions of the modals. The first condition raises philosophical issues, but by following through on a suggestion made by Goodman and endorsed by White,* I think my account meets the condition in a natural and not too tendentious way. The root idea is that necessity (expressed by 'must') is to be understood as conformity with some law, and, a fortiori, possibility (expressed by 'can') is to be understood as nonincompatibility with some law or set of laws. The statement of a law is a generalization that sustains contrary-to-fact and subjunctive conditionals.

So, a first approximation to a definition of 'n must v' might be constructed with the following crude symbolization. Treat 'Fn' as a proposition about an object n. 'F' is a dummy predicate; it is the name of a property in the extended philosophical sense of 'property' according to which, in any true proposition 'Fn', 'F' signifies some property of n. 'F' can stand for a predicate of any degree of length or complexity. (Thus, the behavior of a thing, what it does [past, present, or future], is a property of the thing.) To avoid a circularity in the definitions we shall suppose that 'F' never stands for an overt or covert modal expression. I shall speak of 'Fn' being true or false, and also, if 'Fn' is true, I shall say that F is some Fact (always capitalized) about n. Next correlate 'V' with the 'v' of 'n v', treating 'V' as a predicate form of 'v'. And for simplicity's sake, suppose that any law can be expressed in the form: $(x)(Fx \dot\supset Vx)$. The dot over the horseshoe indicates that the relation is by law and not merely material implication. Given all this, the first approximation to a definition of 'n must v' might be: Fn and $(x)(Fx \dot\supset Vx)$. In other words, to say that n must v is to say that n has some property which

---

is such that it follows by law that 'n v' is true. A corresponding definition of 'n can v' would be derivable through the equivalence of 'n can v' to '—(n must—v)'.

This won't do. It doesn't meet the second condition of an adequate definition: the definiens must have all and only the logical relations possessed by the definiendum. Witness the following cases:

(20)   You can add every integer to every other integer.
(21)   You can't add every integer to every other integer.
(22)   You can take a plane to Nome.
(23)   You can't take a plane to Nome.
(24)   You can break your promise to see Fred.
(25)   You can't break your promise to see Fred.

The members of each pair can be used in a way so that they are contradictories, and also in a way so that they are not. This is not due to other components in the sentences (e.g., a shift from the definite to the indefinite use of 'you'.) To see how the members of each pair can be simultaneously true (or false), associate the following remarks with the original utterances.

(20a)   It's permissible by the rules of arithmetic.
(21a)   Some computations are so long you wouldn't be able to complete them in a billion years.
(22a)   An airport has just been constructed.
(23a)   The cost of the trip would break your bank account.
(24a)   It's easy; all you have to do is just not see him.
(25a)   He's been depending upon you completely.

Furthermore, intuitively one supposes that:

'n must v' entails 'n v' and both entail 'n can v'.
'n cannot v' entails and is entailed by '—(n can v)',
and both entail '—(n v)'.

Yet, these relations appear to break down.

(26) A: This box must contain six ounces of prunes. I just got finished packing and weighing it myself. There was no room for error.

    B: But it can't contain six ounces of prunes. The new government regulations expressly forbid all except four and twelve ounce contents. You had better remove two ounces.

(27) C: I don't remember his name.

    D: But you must remember his name. If we can't produce him as a witness we don't have a leg to stand on in court.

    C: Yes, I realize that I must, but I just can't remember his name.

(28) E: You can't treat him that way; he's a human being!

    F: What do you mean I can't? *I am!*

The same problems arise with 'ought'.

(29)   We ought to arrive before six.

(30)   We ought not to arrive before six.

(29a)   The train is running on schedule.

(30a)   We agreed that we wouldn't.*

Such facts suggest that 'must', 'can', and 'ought' are ambiguous. But to develop that hypothesis would require a counting and a characterization of the various senses. We had a glimpse of what happens when this is tried with 'ought'. What emerged from an attempted delineation of the moral from the nonmoral sense was an examination of our beliefs about which propositions of the form 'n ought to v' are true,

---

* I refrain from exhibiting the apparent breakdown of the entailment relations between 'ought' and 'must', 'can' and 'is', because I have yet to establish which, if any, entailments hold.

not which are meaningful. Instead of producing a semantic characterization of the moral sense of 'ought', we wound up investigating some of the characteristics of a reasonable moral code. This performance would be repeated if one tried to distinguish the allegedly distinct senses of 'must' or 'can'. For example, if one tried to distinguish the 'can' connected with 20a from the 'can' connected with 21a, one would harvest, not a delineation of two senses of 'can', but a distinction between logical possibility and physical possibility. This in turn would lead to a characterization of two different systems of laws. For 20a one would produce a (partial) characterization of a system of mathematical laws, and for 21a a scientific theory about living organisms. (As I read him, this is one of the lessons of Quine's 'Two Dogmas of Empiricism'.)

This divorce of intention and consequence suggests an alternative conception of the modals which I shall now go on to develop. I take the modals to be univocal and describe their anomalous behavior in terms, not of different senses, but of their employment in connection with various more or less independent systems of laws. Since my account possesses all the virtues of any ambiguist account I know of, its preference is warranted by Occam's eraser, and as I proceed some deeper and more interesting grounds for electing my account will appear.

I shall be using the word 'System' (always capitalized) to mean a more or less well organized and integrated system of laws (and perhaps other propositions as well) concerning some more or less well-defined set of properties of some more or less well-defined set of objects. By itself, this definition does not express what I have in mind with the term 'System'. More needs to be said, but less than one might suppose, for

The Meanings of the Modals

the gist of my account is that the features of Systems are irrelevant to the meanings of the modals per se.

The term 'System' need not mislead; but at times the word 'Theory' would be better, so I will use it (always capitalized) interchangeably with 'System'. According to my definition, all of the following count as Systems: a scientific theory, a code of etiquette or morals, a mathematical system, a language (i.e., the system of phonological, semantical, and syntactical rules), a game, a legal system (i.e., the system of rules or laws), a man's system of beliefs (better: propositions expressing the beliefs) about the physical world or actual or rational human behavior, and so on. My definition of 'System' is intentionally quite broad and somewhat vague in order to encompass this variety. I believe that the definition is not so broad as to include any unwanted items, but if it is too broad or too narrow the definition will have to be amended. I am of the conviction that, if necessary, this could be done, since I am of the conviction that the sorts of things I mean to include form a natural class.

Some further definitions may dispel much of the initial bewilderment about Systems. I call a System a System of Actuality (hereafter, SA) if, when it contains some law '(x) $(Fx \supset Vx)$' and a case is discovered in which '$Fn.-Vn$' is true, then the law is judged to be wrong. A scientific theory is a paradigm of an SA. I call a System a System of Ideality (hereafter, SI) if, when it contains some law '(x) $(Fx \supset Vx)$' and a case is discovered in which '$Fn.-Vn$' is true, then $-Vn$ (the state of affairs or action, not the proposition) is judged to be wrong. A moral code is a paradigm of an SI. The laws of an SI, as I am conceiving them, have the same form as those of an SA. For example, a moral law (i.e., a law belonging to some moral System) might be: If a man m murders another man, then m is punished. If it is of any help, one might think of these laws in Kantian terms as descriptions of the behavior of objects with a holy will, but one need not resort to fictions in order to properly construe such laws. Their meaning is as literal and their proper interpretation as straightforward as the statements of the laws of an SA; it is only some philosophical preconceptions that make it look otherwise. An unprejudiced review of the practices of our speech community shows that I am merely putting all the laws of SI's into a form that many of them already possess.

Having it close to hand, I read in the Harvard University "Supplement to the General Announcement on Higher Degrees in Philosophy": "The completed thesis is read and appraised by a committee of two, usually identical with the candidate's Thesis Advisory Committee" (p. 5). The author of this statement is writing quite properly, but shall we say he is mistaken, since, as is common knowledge, sometimes a thesis is not read and appraised by a committee of two? Often one, and sometimes both advisors do not read the thesis in its entirety, and in some cases they do not read it at all, nor does some substitute. Shall we suppose that the author is unaware of this, that he is naive? Pish and pshaw! Clearly, the writer does not mean to be describing a regularity in the actual behavior of thesis advisors, and thus what he says is not falsified by a deviation from such a regularity. Rather he is saying what advisors do if they act in conformity with the rules of a certain institution (System). Which rules?— Principally the one he is now stating. If some advisor does not act accordingly, we do not judge the author to be wrong in saying what he says, but the advisor in doing what he does. Thus, in an SA, an utterance of 'n v' (not the sentence it-

The Meanings of the Modals

self) is to be understood to mean that *in fact* n v; in an SI, an utterance of 'n v' is to be understood to mean that *ideally* n v, that is, it is (or would be) wrong if in fact −(n v). Note further than an unproblematic sense can be given to the idea that the laws of an SI sustain contrary-to-fact and subjunctive conditionals. For if what the author says is true, then it is also true that if my mother had written a thesis, it would have been read and appraised by a committee of two, etc. If that counterfactual is false, then her advisors would have been doing something wrong. And if that law were understood in the context of an SA and the counterfactual were false, it would follow that the purported law was not a law, that is, that the law is wrong. (An oversimplification lurks here, but will be removed in a while.)

The definitions of an SA and an SI are designed to capture a long-recognized distinction between two sorts of things we call laws. The distinction is expressed in terms of two ways of treating a law. The difference is not a linguistic one; the same grammatical form and the same vocabulary, even the very same unambiguous sentence, can (not must) be used to state a law of an SA and a law of an SI. The difference lies, not in the expression of the law, but in what is done with the law. So I see no reason for calling 'law' or 'System', as I use them, ambiguous. One could as well say that 'statute' is ambiguous because some statutes are treated with respect and generally enforced and obeyed, and some are not. Admittedly, it is a contingent matter whether a particular statute is treated with respect and generally enforced and obeyed. But so too, it is not a semantic question whether a particular kind of System is an SA or an SI, and neither is it a semantic question whether an *adequate* System of a particular kind is an

91

SA or an SI. (See pp. 140–148) And as for the word 'wrong' which appears in both definitions, Chapter Five should squash any charge that it is ambiguous.

According to my account, to say 'n ought to v' (or 'n must v' or 'n cannot v') is to say, among other things, that there *exists* an *adequate relevant* System. This requires clarification. First, let me distinguish between a *specific* System and a *kind* of System. Moral codes and scientific theories are different kinds of Systems. So too, a scientific theory of light propagation is a different kind of System from a scientific theory of sexual reproduction. There may be many specific Systems of the same kind: Bushido and the Quaker morality are both moral Systems; Copernican and Ptolemaic theories are both astronomical Theories.

The *adequacy* of a specific System must be judged in terms of the kind of System it is. The criteria of adequacy are relative to the kind of System being evaluated. I confess to being incapable of answering most of the serious questions about evaluating Systems. Fortunately this is no handicap since such matters have nothing to do with the meanings of the modals. The notion of adequacy enters the definitions only to ensure that the purported laws on which a modal proposition rests are genuine laws. Two further points about adequacy. First, the use of the modals does not seem to presuppose that no more than one System of each kind can be adequate. Second, though 'adequate' might be called a normative term, it is not an overt modal term, nor does it seem to require a modal in its definition. Thus, its appearance in the definitions does not threaten their noncircularity.

To say that an adequate System of a kind *exists* does not mean that the System has been discovered or invented. To say that such a System does *not* exist is comparable to saying that there does not exist a 5 in the decimal expansion of 1/3. The latter claim may be paraphrased by saying that no matter how far one carried the expansion, one would never come across a 5. Similarly, the former claim may be paraphrased by saying that no matter what propositions one uttered, one would never state an adequate System of the kind in question. To say that an adequate System of a certain kind exists is just to deny that one does not exist. Radical moral skepticism is the thesis that no adequate moral System exists, and radical skepticism about the physical world claims that no adequate scientific System exists. The existence of unknown adequate Systems is required in order to allow a modal proposition like 'Nothing can travel faster than the speed of light.' to have an eternal (or timeless) truth-value just as other propositions do. Suppose that Einsteinian Theory is adequate and that it sustains that proposition. But if the world had blown up in 1901, the truth-value of that proposition would have been unaffected. I doubt that such talk commits me to acknowledge the existence of a Platonic realm of adequate Systems, but if it does, so be it.

The notion of *relevance* is at the nub of my account. Take the sentence:

(31)   The box cannot contain six ounces of prunes.

Sentence 31 is used in speeches 31A and 31I to form different propositions.

(31A)   It just can't be done, I tell you. The box cannot contain six ounces of prunes. Even if you pitted, mashed, and compressed them, you still couldn't fit six ounces of prunes into it.

(31I)   I don't care how much trouble it causes. The box cannot contain six ounces of prunes. The new government regulation expressly forbids all except four and twelve ounce containers. Your job is to make sure that the regulation is complied with.

According to my account, the multiple propositional potential of sentence 31 is attributable to certain variables appearing in the definition of 'n cannot v'. The principal variable ranges over kinds of Systems in connection with which the sentence can be used. Which System is the relevant System is determined by the speaker, his intentions. Because the sentence can be meant and interpreted in terms of two or more kinds of Systems, the same sentence can be used to form two or more different propositions (or illocutions) that may differ in their truth-value.

It is important to distinguish three different matters here: first, the meaning of *sentence* 31; second, the truth-conditions of the correlative *propositions* in 31A and 31I; third, the way in which an audience determines which kind of System is relevant, and, thereby, which proposition is being formed by an utterance of 31. The meaning of sentence 31 is expressable by a definition consisting of four conjuncts, one of which is, 'There exists an adequate relevant System.', The meaning of sentence 31 makes no reference to any specific System or kind of System. 'Cannot' can operate in connection with any kind of System; it is System-neutral.

Like any sentence, 31 does not have a truth-value. The sentence is used to form one proposition in 31A and a different one in 31I. The truth-conditions of these propositions are given by the definition of 31. According to that definition, these propositions are true only if there exists an adequate relevant System, but the definition does not specify which

The Meanings of the Modals

System is relevant. The relevance of a System is determined by the speaker's intentions, and since the speakers of 31A and 31I obviously have different Systems in mind, they are forming two different propositions which may differ in truth-value.

For a speaker to mean (intend, have in mind) some System, he need not actively think about the System. Nor need he be able to say much about the System or even know what a System is. To say that he has a certain System in mind is only to say that he is inclined to give or accept certain kinds of reasons in support or criticism of his utterance, and to regard other kinds of reasons as irrelevant. If he is unable to do such things even in a rough-and-ready way, then the truth of what he says cannot be assessed, for there is no way to determine what, if anything, he means. He may or may not have a *specific* System in mind, but he must have a *kind* of System in mind even if it be a very broad kind. If the specific System he has in mind is inadequate, what he says may still be true if some adequate System of that kind supports his claim. But we would judge his claim to be false if the only adequate Systems which would support a proposition formed from the uttered sentence are of a different kind from the one he has in mind (i.e., they are irrelevant). If he does not have even a kind of System in mind, then one is inclined to say that he is misusing words; the sentence that he utters has a meaning, but he does not mean anything by those words. It would be like using a referring expression without having any referent in mind.

In consequence of all this, all the entailment relations of a modal proposition hold if and only if * the propositions in

---

* If (some of) the laws of one System are used within another System, the entailment relations may hold even though two Systems are involved. For instance, since the laws of logic are used within any ade-

the antecedent and consequent have the same relevant System. The breakdown of those relations illustrated by propositions 20–30 was due to different kinds of Systems being assigned to the different propositions. (N.B.: 'n v' must also be understood in terms of the relevant System, and its interpretation depends on whether an SA or an SI is meant.) Thus a modal proposition neither entails nor is entailed by any proposition connected with a different System, for the relation between them cannot be purely semantic. Instead, whether any implications between them hold at all turns on issues internal to one or both Systems; it is a problem of Theory construction, not high-level lexicography. A case in point is the relation of 'ought' to 'can'. It is not a semantic issue and cannot be decided on semantic grounds whether 'n cannot v' implies '—(n ought to v)' when the former is connected to a physical System and the latter to a moral one. Whether that implication holds can only be a question about the contents of an adequate moral System—and the modals tell us nothing about the contents of any System (except, of course, our language). There is a genuine problem here—or rather, a cluster of problems—but the issues are matters of justice and utility, not language, and thus not relevant to my present task.*

Sometimes the contents of the 'n' and 'v' of a modal proposition are sufficient clues as to the relevant System. Sometimes the speech context provides further clues. But sometimes these clues are insufficient, and the audience must ask

---

quate scientific Theory, 'n (logically) cannot v' entails 'n (physically) cannot v'. One could say that the laws of one System (e.g., physics) *include* the laws of the other (e.g., logic).

* Hereafter, unless explicit exception is made, whenever I discuss the relations between two modal propositions, both propositions are connected to the same System.

The Meanings of the Modals

the speaker what he has in mind. In 31A and 31I we can spot the relevant System by the speech context. How? In 31I there is a fairly explicit reference to a particular System. The government regulation mentioned presumably belongs to a System of such regulations (laws). In 31A, though the Theory is in no way mentioned, it is indicated by the details of the speech. We are led to suppose that the modal proposition is true in virtue of the size of the box ('It's too small.') and certain laws about the density of prunes ('Even if you pitted, mashed, and compressed them. . . .'). So, plainly the relevant System is a physical Theory.

But why is it so plain that the relevant System is a physical System? It is not because of the meaning of 'cannot', and neither is it because of the meanings of any of the other words in the whole of 31A. Nor is it simply that we assume that the speaker is speaking rationally and coherently, for that only begs the question of why we suppose that a physical Theory is the relevant one. Rather, the operative assumption here is that the speaker largely shares our conceptual scheme, our total system of beliefs. Let us take a simpler and more extreme case to make this point clear.

If someone were to say to us:

(35)   Nothing can travel faster than the speed of light.

we would assume straightaway that the relevant System is a physical Theory. Yet I suppose it is possible that the speaker belongs to a community with a bizarre code of etiquette according to which it is impolite to travel that fast. But I do not suppose that the people I talk to belong to that community. We would continue to suppose that the relevant System is a physical one unless and until we had reason to suppose that the speaker's conceptual system is radically different from ours. But note, we do not need to assume that 35 is true in order to interpret it. That is, we do not need to suppose that some adequate physical System supports that claim. We need only suppose that if any kind of adequate System *might* serve as a support for that claim, it would have to be a physical System. But to know that this is so, one must know a great deal more than the meanings of words.

I am saying that it is because of certain beliefs, not because of the meanings of the modals or other words that we naturally use and interpret certain sentences in connection with one kind of System and not another. If someone says 'The roast ought to be done by now.' we know straight off that the relevant System is a physical, not a moral one. We know this not because the utterance would be ungrammatical if a moral System were intended, but because we know that the speaker could not seriously suppose that anything but a physical System could be adequate and still support that claim. Given our conceptual scheme, some sentences will be naturally associated with more than one kind of System, and some will be naturally associated with only one kind of System, and some will not be naturally associated with any kind of System. The first type of sentence will strike us as ambiguous; the second as unproblematically univocal; and the third as odd—but they should not be thought to be ungrammatical.*

---

* Though 'must', 'can', and 'ought' can now be used in connection with any kind of System, this was not always so. At one time 'can' was used more or less exclusively with SA's, not with SI's. (Some speakers persist in this, and thus they refuse to interchange 'can' with 'may'.) Perhaps as a result, when the context of an utterance with 'can' leaves open whether an SA or an SI is meant, our first impulse is usually to suppose that an SA is meant. The different nuances of 'ought' and 'shought' may also be attributed to their histories. Perhaps because

The Meanings of the Modals

The choice of relevant System may have subtle effects on the interpretation of an utterance. For example, an utterance of

(36)   Every contestant can win.

might be (a) a statement of the rules of the contest, (b) a tautology: Every one who is eligible to win is eligible to win, or (c) an empirical claim about the equality of ability of the competitors. An instantiation of 36:

(37)   He can win.

is similarly interpretable. Most commonly 37 would be used as an implicit denial of 36c, and thus suggests that there is some substantial probability, not a mere possibility, that he will win. But 'can' does not shift senses. The relevant System for 36c and 37c encompasses not only the rules of the contest (as do 36b and 37b), but also the physical laws concerning the attributes of the players, and thus 37c can be truly asserted only of those contestants who have a real chance of winning.

By arranging the pieces produced so far we get a second approximation to a definition of 'n must v':

(j)   There exists an adequate relevant System y; and
(jj)   n has the property F; and,

'shought' continues to be related to 'shall', it has a stronger flavor of 'shall' (or 'will' or 'is') than 'ought' has, and thus is more comfortably used and readily interpreted in connection with SA's than is 'ought', which is most comfortably used and readily interpreted in connection with SI's, especially moral ones. (Meta-ethicists may make of such facts what they will.) With 'must' and 'must not' the matter is more complex. (See pp. 107–109.)

(jjj)   according to y, F is such that if 'Fn' is true then 'n v' is true.

And we get a second approximation to a definition of 'n can v':

(1)   There does not exist an adequate relevant System y; or

(ll)   there does not exist a property F which is such that both 'Fn' is true, and, according to y, if 'Fn' is true then '—(n v)' is true.

But a definition of 'ought' can't be concocted out of these ingredients. In order to supply the missing bit I must refine some of my earlier remarks.

I said (pp. 89–91) that when we are confronted with a deviation from a law of an SA we judge the law to be wrong, but when confronted with a deviation from a law of an SI we judge the deviation to be wrong. But in neither case is this always strictly true. As recent research in the history and philosophy of science has amply documented, in an SA such as a physical Theory a single untoward event, even if rep-licatable, is rarely treated as a good ground for abandoning an otherwise well-established law. Anomalous incidents may be deprived of falsifying force for various reasons and by various means. For one thing, laws cannot be tried indi-vidually; it is always some substantial subset of a System that is being tested and this provides the scientist with consider-able play. For another thing, the statements of the laws are, in one way or another, idealizations of reality, and, in con-sequence, theoretical prediction may not unremittingly gibe with observed data. An example is the laws derived from the smoothest curve plotted by a series of experiments: e.g., At standard pressure, water boils at 212°F. A sane scientist is not likely to discard that law upon discovery of an instance in which water boiled at 213°F, even if his most earnest efforts confirmed that the water was pure, the pressure standard, and so forth. As a last resort the scientist may just reserve judgment on the matter and hope that someday a happy explanation will be hit upon. A parallel feature is to be found in some SI's. There too a System may allow for circumstances (some of which are called extenuating) being such that noncompliance with a law is not a ground for judging the act to be wrong.

The details of all this need not detain us; they are matters of the innards of each System. The essential point is that many Systems, SA's and SI's alike, contain mechanisms permitting divagations from the laws to be treated in ways other than those I first described. These mechanisms are, in effect, compensatory; they are found in Systems in which we lack full advance knowledge or control of the relevant factors affecting the accuracy of the laws in particular cases.* Thus, they are present in physical, moral, aesthetic, and prudential (e.g., skill, strategy) Systems, and are absent from legal, quasi-legal (e.g., games), and logical Systems. This is of interest because 'ought' is freely and regularly used in the former Systems, but is rarely or restrictedly used with the latter ones. And this correspondence suggests that 'ought' expresses the relationship that necessitates the use of those mechanisms— a suggestion I accept and will develop.

These considerations lead me to introduce a somewhat curious term. Though I define it here, I shall not now do much in the way of explanation since the import of the term does not become manifest until the defense of the defi-

---

* I am not wholly satisfied with the description of the missing feature, but I think it will suffice.

The Significance of Sense

nition of 'ought'. I shall use the expression, 'Circumstances, C' or sometimes simply 'C'. It can be understood through its extensional equivalence to: According to the System y, if n has a property F which is such that '$(x)(Fx \supset Vx)$' is a law of y, then 'n v' is true. The idea being expressed here is that C is the Circumstances in which, according to the relevant System, '$(x)(Fx \supset Vx)$' accurately determines whether 'n v' is true, when 'Fn' is true.

With this term, improved definitions of 'SA' and 'SI' can be provided. A System y is an SA if and only if, when n has a property F which is such that '$(x)(Fx \supset Vx)$' is a law of y, and the Circumstances C obtain, but 'n v' is false, then '$(x)(Fx \supset Vx)$' is judged to be wrong. A system y is an SI if and only if, when n has a property F which is such that '$(x)(Fx \supset Vx)$' is a law of y, and C obtains, but 'n v' is false (i.e., '$-(n\ v)$' is true), then $-(n\ v)$ is judged to be wrong.* I shall use this as the formal definition of 'SA' and 'SI', but it is perhaps somewhat misleading since the difference is defined in terms of violations of a law. Actually the distinction turns on the relation of a law to both instances and counterinstances to a law: in an SI the law is used as a ground for assessing both instances and counterinstances to the law; in an SA the instances and counterinstances are used as grounds for assessing the law. Note finally that even if this characterization of an SA and an SI is unsatisfactory,

---

* A glance back at the definition of 'C' reveals a redundancy in the definitions of 'SA' and 'SI'. However, though C obtains if and only if, according to y, a certain lawful relation obtains, I am not using 'C' to refer to that lawful relation as such. Rather I mean to be referring to a circumstance or situation, the contents of which are picked out by the System. The redundancy is extensional, not intensional, and serves to segregate some separate features. It recurs in my definitions of the modals.

my definitions of 'must', 'can', and 'ought' are unaffected, because the distinction does not enter into the definitions themselves. The problems about the nature of an SA and an SI are problems about certain kinds of Systems, not about the meanings of 'ought', 'can', or 'must'.

And now, the definitions. I begin with 'must'. Take the sentence:

(38)   Bly must die.

The definition of sentence 38 consists of four conjuncts: *

(j)   There exists an adequate relevant System y; and
(jj)   there is some Fact F about Bly (i.e., 'Fn' is true); and,
(jjj)   according to y, F is such that if Bly is F and the Circumstances C obtain, then Bly dies (i.e., 'n v' is true); and
(jjjj) the Circumstances C obtain.

A proposition formed from 38 is true if and only if each of the four conjuncts j-jjjj is true, and if any are false, then the proposition is false, but not meaningless. There may well be alternative and even superior ways of defining 38. I chose these four conjuncts because they correspond to four distinct ways of showing a proposition of the form 'n must v' to be false.

Let me illustrate this four-fold path to falsehood. Suppose you thought that Bly must die because you thought that Bly swallowed lye, but Bly did not swallow lye and neither is there anything else which would cause Bly to die, so jj is false, and hence 38 is false. Or, you thought Bly must

---

* Sentences are not commonly said to have definitions, but that should not be an obstacle to understanding here.

die because you rightly thought that Bly swallowed lye, but Bly swallowed a lye antidote (rye), so jjjj is false, and hence 38 is false. Or, you thought Bly must die because you rightly thought that Bly swallowed lye but not a lye antidote, but lye is not lethal, so jjj is false, and hence 38 is false. Or, you thought that Bly must die because you rightly thought that Bly swallowed lye but not rye, and that, according to the best available medical Theories, lye is lethal, but in fact there does not exist an adequate System regarding lye, so j is false, and hence 38 is false.

The definition of 'n must v' also serves as the definition of 'n has to v', and 'n has got to v',* since both are synonymous with 'n must v'. Further, 'n does not have to v', 'n has not got to v', and 'n need not v' are all definable as '—(n must v)' since they are three alternative ways of saying what is almost never expressed by saying 'It is not the case that n must v'.

If this is an adequate definition of 'n must v', then it is natural to define 'n must not v' as:

(k)   There exists an adequate relevant System y; and
(kk)   'Fn' is true (i.e., there is some Fact F about n); and
(kkk)   according to y, F is such that if 'Fn' is true and C obtains, then 'n v' is false (i.e., —(n v) is true); and
(kkkk)   C obtains.

That is, the definition of 'n must not v' differs from that of 'n must v' solely by having 'n v' negated. Yet it is equally natural to use k-kkkk as the definition of 'n cannot v'. This is

---

* I shall ignore the task of specifying the relevant uses of these expressions. Obviously the definition does not apply to such cases as 'The issue has to do with a matter of grave concern.'. Even ignoring such uses, 'have to', 'have got to', and 'must' have their differences. For example, 'have to' can be preceded by 'will'; 'have got to' and 'must' cannot: 'We will have to see him tomorrow.'.

troublesome since 'must not' seems different from 'cannot'.
Compare:

(39)   You must not satisfy her boundless lust.
(40)   You cannot satisfy her boundless lust.

Nevertheless I shall contend that k-kkkk serves as an adequate
definition of both 'n must not v' and 'n cannot v'. The differences between these sentences are to be understood as
being unexpressed by their proper definitions, though explicable in terms of them. (See pp. 107–109.)

By accepting the definition of 'n cannot v' and the undeniable truth of ''—(n cannot v)' ≡ 'n can v' ' one is led to
define 'n can v' by three disjuncts.

(1)   There does not exist an adequate relevant System
        y; or
(ll)   there does not exist a property F such that both 'Fn'
        is true, and, according to y, if 'Fn' is true and the
        Circumstances C obtain, then '—(n v)' is true; or
(lll)   C does not obtain.

At first glimpse this looks unappealing as a definition of 'n
can v', but upon closer inspection it will be seen to serve
nicely. A proposition of the form 'n can v' is true if and only
if one of the three disjuncts l-lll is true.

First, n can v if there does not exist an adequate relevant
System. Disjunct 1 is true only if the relevant form of radical
skepticism is correct. Note that even if radical moral skepticism is correct, emotivism and many other forms of noncognitivism are still ruled out. Rather than M-criterion modal
moral judgments being pseudo judgments, some species of
utterance lacking genuine truth-values, they have a quite elegant truth calculus; their truth-value is a function of there

being no adequate moral System. All affirmative judgments with 'must', 'must not', 'cannot', and (as we shall see) 'ought' and 'ought not' are false and hence all their negations and all affirmative moral judgments with 'can' are true. In this situation, the truth of 'n can v' follows from there being no (such thing as a) good reason of a certain sort (i.e., a moral reason) for n not to v. This is unquestionably the most natural interpretation of moral skepticism. It is the consequence that concerns people. What Kirilov hopes (and fears) is that 'Everything is permitted.' is true, not that 'Something is not permitted.' is an ungrammatical sentence or lacks a genuine truth-value.

The second disjunct, ll, expresses the idea most immediately associated with 'can'. It is the negation of the conjunction of kk and kkk of the definition of 'cannot'. In essence it says that, according to the relevant adequate System, the properties possessed by n when conjoined with the Circumstances C are compatible with the truth of 'n v'.

The third disjunct, lll, expresses the idea that n can v when the Circumstances are such that the laws of the relevant adequate System do not accurately determine whether 'n v' is true. Different kinds of Systems present different kinds of cases here. Apparently, an adequate physical Theory is unable to forecast some subatomic events. Thus, it might be true to say of some set of electrons that 95 per cent of them cannot move to a certain ring, but false to say of any particular member of the set that it cannot move to the ring. In the sphere of morality it would generally be conceded by all but the intolerant objectivists among us that in some cases one exhausts the capacities of an adequate moral System without producing a conclusive decision. Where there are good but

The Meanings of the Modals

not sufficient reasons for both performing some act and not performing it (i.e., for 'n v' and '—(n v)'), then all one can properly say is 'n can v' (or 'n can —v'). Normally the conflict is between performing a specific act v and performing some other specific act u which is incompatible with v. Here one can say, 'n can v and n can u, but n must v or u'.

As with 'must', other accounts of 'can' may be acceptable and even preferable to mine. I opted for my definition because the three disjuncts correspond to three defenses of a proposition of the form 'n can v' which are distinct and exhaust the possibilities. (Alternatively, 'n can v' is true if and only if any one of the four conjuncts k-kkkk is false.)

My definition of 'can' takes a somewhat negative form compared to my definitions of 'must', 'must not', 'cannot', and (as we shall see) 'ought' and 'ought not'. The definitions thereby reflect what I take to be a feature of our conceptual scheme. In general we assume a phenomenon is possible unless something prevents it. This is in opposition to thinking that a thing is impossible until the obstacles to it are removed or that a thing is necessary until the compelling forces are stayed. The analogue to this in morality and some other Systems of Ideality is that a man is free to do anything unless and until there is sufficient reason not to. (All this has important and complex connections with our conception of human agency and free will.)

Moreover, I believe such facts help explain most of the differences between 'must not' and 'cannot'. Note, 'n cannot v' is understood as the sentential negation of 'n can v', whereas 'n must not v' is the modal negation of 'n must v'. A natural paraphrase of 'n cannot v' is 'Not possibly (or, Impossibly) n v', whereas the comparable paraphrase of 'n must

The Significance of Sense

not v' is 'Necessarily not n v' or 'Necessarily n—v'.* This difference makes a difference. The question 'can or cannot?' is a far more natural and normal question than either 'must or must not?' or 'must not or not must not?'. Witness for example the plethora of terms in our vocabulary that we would naturally associate with the notion of impossibility: 'obstacle', 'prevent', 'implacable', 'disable', 'obstruct', 'unsolvable', 'impede', 'immovable', etc. Contrast this with the paucity of terms we would naturally associate with the curious complex notion, necessary-that-not.

When these facts are tied to principles of discourse they reduce, if not remove, the paradoxical character of my equation of 'must not' and 'cannot'. I would suppose it to be a rule of speech that when denying a proposition, whether 'must not' or 'cannot' is used will depend on what is being denied. If it is 'n can v', one uses 'cannot', not 'must not'. But also, when denying 'The substance is soluble in water.', one uses 'The substance cannot dissolve in water.', not 'The

---

* Actually, what I have called modal negation covers two different functions, negation of the modal itself: 'n mustn't v', and negation of the predicate: 'n must —v'. The difference exists and is more clearly expressible with 'ought not'; we can say either 'n ought not (or, oughtn't) to v' or 'n ought to not v'. This difference is comparable to that in nonmodal sentences between '—(n v)' and 'n —v'. I have used the former in the definitions of 'must not' and 'ought not', but the latter should be used in cases of predicative negation. Ordinarily this difference doesn't make much difference, but it can. Thus, 'n must v or n must not v' is ambiguous. It is interpretable as either the logical truth 'n must (v or —v)' which presupposes the law '(x)(Fx⊃ — (Vx. — Vx)' and is compatible with 'n can v and n can —v', or as 'n must v or n mustn't v' which presupposes that the relevant System contains either '(x)(Fx⊃Vx)' or '(x)(Fx⊃ — Vx)' and is thus incompatible with 'n can v and n can —v'. (The same point can be made with 'ought not'.) However, 'cannot' serves only as a sentential negation. Note that 'n cannot (or, can't) v' is the contradictory of 'n can v', while 'n can —v' is its subcontrary.

The Meanings of the Modals

substance must not dissolve in water.' Extending this idea to cases other than denial brings us to the nub of the problem. Roughly, we use 'cannot' when we suppose the falsity of 'n v' is due to some obstruction or *lack* of power, ability, right, or the like. And, again roughly, where we tend to think in terms of there being some *positive* reason for the falsity of 'n v', we would tend to use 'must not'. 'Must not' is more naturally associated with SI's because there an act may be positively prohibited, not just prevented. In SA's its most common use is that of expressing the relation of a conclusion '—(n v)' to certain premises. If I say, 'Max must not be here because if he were he would have contacted us.', my claim should be paraphrased by 'Necessarily, if not P (Max contacts us), then not n v (Max is here)', not by 'Necessarily not n v'. (Note that my definitions cover this kind of case.) Here too, 'must not' does not oppose 'can' directly, as does 'cannot'. Obviously much more needs to be said about 'must not' and 'cannot', but perhaps enough has been said to let us move on to 'ought'.

The definition of 'n ought to v' can now be stated; it consists of three conjuncts:

(m)   There exists an adequate relevant System y; and
(mm)   there exists a property F such that 'Fn' is true; and,
(mmm) according to y, F is such that if 'Fn' is true and C obtains then 'n v' is true.

The definition of 'n ought to v' is the same as that of 'n must v' without the conjunct jjjj (i.e., C obtains). Correspondingly, the definition of 'n ought not to v' is the same as that of 'n must not v' and 'n cannot v' minus the conjunct kkkk (i.e., C obtains). So, the definition of 'n ought not to v' differs from that of 'n ought to v' solely by having 'n v' negated.* In consequence 'n must v' entails but is not entailed by 'n ought to v', and 'n must not v' and 'n cannot v' entail 'n ought not to v' but are not entailed by it. Further, while 'n must v' entails 'n v' and both 'n must not v' and 'n cannot v' entail '— (n v)', 'n ought to v' does not entail 'n v' and 'n ought not to v' does not entail '— (n v). Instead, 'n ought to v' entails 'n v or C does not obtain', and 'n ought not to v' entails '— (n v) or — (C obtains)'. The task now is to establish that these definitions and their relations accurately map the actual usage of these words.

Examine the following utterances, remembering at all times to keep the relevant System constant within the utterance.

(41)   You don't have to see him, but you must.

(42)   You don't have to see him, but you ought to.

(43)   You must see him, but you ought not to.

(44)   You must see him, but it's not the case that you ought to.

(45)   You must not see him, but you ought to.

(46)   You cannot see him, but you ought to.

(47)   You can see him and you ought to.

All but 42 and 47 sound logically odd. This seems sufficient warrant for saying that 'n must v' entails but is not entailed by 'n ought to v', and that 'n must not v' and 'n cannot v'

---

* An oversimplification. In practice, 'ought not' is both the modal negation of 'ought' (as 'must not' is of 'must') and the sentential negation (as 'cannot' is of 'can'). This is probably due to the awkwardness of saying 'It is not the case that n ought to v' and the lack of alternative ways of saying that. By contrast 'must not' need not do duty as a sentential negation because other expressions (e.g., 'need not') are available. For clarity, I shall treat 'n ought not to v' solely as the modal negation, and shall use '— (n ought to v)' as the sole sentential negation.

entail but are not entailed by 'n ought not to v'. This explains and is further confirmed by such common utterances as.

(48)   Not only ought you to do it, you must do it!

(49)   It's not just that you ought to do it; you've got to do it!

As for the relation of 'n ought to v' to 'n v', compare:

(50)   That's funny. The roast ought to be done by now. I wonder why it isn't.

(51)   That's funny. The roast must be done by now. I wonder why it isn't.

(52)   This car ought not to be getting thirty miles to the gallon, but it is, so let's just be thankful.

(53)   This car cannot (or, must not) be getting thirty miles to the gallon, but it is, so let's just be thankful.

Sentences like 51 and 53 are logically odd; 50 and 52 are not—they are things we commonly say. To be sure we also say things like:

(54)   This is incredible! He must be here . . . yet he isn't!

(55)   Nothing could have gone wrong, yet everything did go wrong!

I submit that utterances like 54 and 55 are acceptable, yet state a paradox. They are used precisely because of that paradox to emphasize the incongruity of the situation described. If one wished to be pedantic, one might get the speaker of 55 to admit that he really meant that it certainly *seemed* that nothing could go wrong. The same applies to 54. But with 50 and 52 no such admission would be forthcoming. In fact, though not ungrammatical, it requires rather special circumstances for one to say something like:

(56)   It seemed that the roast ought to be done by now. I wonder why it isn't.

(57)   It seemed that this car ought not to be getting thirty miles to the gallon, but it is, so let's just be thankful.

The behavior of certain adverbs sheds light on this. Compare:

(58)   You must, you absolutely must do it.

(59)   You ought, you absolutely ought to do it.

(60)   You cannot, you absolutely cannot do it.

(61)   You must not, you absolutely must not do it.

(62)   You ought not, you absolutely ought not to do it.

'Absolutely' goes well with 'must', 'must not', and 'cannot', but sounds odd with 'ought' and 'ought not'. I suggest that this is so because there is nothing absolute about 'ought'; since 'n ought to v' entails 'n v or —(C obtains)', 'ought' bears an aspect of the provisional. In this respect 'ought' is like 'may' and 'might'. Note the strangeness of

(63)   He might, he absolutely might do it.

Still, it needs to be shown that these features of 'ought' stem from the component 'C obtains', that is, that something in ordinary language corresponds to the formula: If n ought to v, and —(n v), then C does not obtain. What seems to fit the bill here is the fact that if 'n ought to v' and '—(n v)' are true, then we can say and it is true that *something must have gone wrong*. Note:

(64)   That's funny. The roast ought to be done by now. I wonder why it isn't. Something must have gone wrong.

(65)   This car ought not to be getting thirty miles to the

gallon, but it is. There must be something wrong, but whatever it is, it's perfectly all right with me.

I submit that what has gone wrong is something falsifying 'C obtains'. One cannot maintain that n ought to v (and hence cannot maintain that n ought to v and that —(n v)) if any of the three conjuncts m-mmm are false. Whether or not 'n v' is true, 'n ought to v' would be simply false if no relevant System were adequate or no Fact F were such that, according to the System, if n is F and the Circumstances C obtain, then 'n v' is true. Assuming that the general form of my account is correct, it would have to be that the embedded 'C obtains' is false.

This line of argument is sustained by an investigation of the details of particular cases. The truth of 64 could not be maintained as a whole if the roast had been put in the oven or the temperature were set at 95°F. Such Facts as that the roast had been in a 325°F oven for at least a half hour per pound must obtain. Similarly, one must not be supposing that it is a law that it takes only ten minutes per pound to roast beef at 325°F. But one can maintain the truth of all of 64 if the gas company had a half-hour shutdown or some chemical delaying cooking time had been inadvertently introduced into the meat.

Thus far I have restricted my examples to cases involving an SA, not because of some important difference with SI's, for there is none, but because my reader may not find the matter as immediately perspicuous with an SI. The same semantic relation holds independently of the relevant System: 'n ought to v, and —(n v)' entails '—(C obtains)'. Of course, in an SI if n is an agent, and 'n ought to v' and 'C obtains' are true while *in fact* —(n v), that will mean that *n* had *done* something wrong. So what we need is a case in which the speaker knows (or firmly believes) that the agent n would not, at least in this instance, do something wrong. That is, while 'n v' is false the agent has not done something wrong, because, though his action violates some law(s) of the System, the Circumstances are such that the System does not lead us to condemn the action. In such a case, if the agent does not do what the speaker says he ought to do, the speaker will suppose that something must have gone wrong.

(66)   Rodney ought to be here by now. He promised me and he is a man of his word. I fear that something must have gone wrong. I only hope that nothing has happened to Rod.

All this might be summed up impressionistically by saying that 'must' means sufficient reasons, whereas 'ought' means good but not sufficient reasons. So, in an SA to say 'He must do it.' is to say that he will do it, no ifs, ands, or buts. But to say 'He ought to do it.' in an SA is to say he will do it if everything goes according to schedule. In an SI, to say 'You must do it.' is to say you will do it, no excuses!, but to say 'You ought to do it.' is to say that you will do it or if you don't, you'd better have an excuse.

To get beyond impressionism, the claim 'C obtains' must be given more attention. It needs saying that no sharp line separates those features of a total state of affairs properly covered by the 'F' term from those properly covered by the 'C' term. Distinguishing the Facts from the Circumstances is similar to, for it is of a piece with, picking out one factor in a set of conditions as the *cause* of a particular event. In a physical Theory, what I call the Facts would be called the cause, and what I call the Circumstances would encompass the remaining necessary conditions. In a moral System, the Facts are those factors justifying the performance of an act, and the Circumstances encompass those factors whose absence excuses one from the performance. Admittedly, I am foggy about the details of the principles used in distinguishing the cause from the rest of the necessary conditions and the justifying conditions from the excusing conditions. Fortunately, my ignorance is innocuous, for this is a matter internal to the different Systems. As far as the semantic issues go, it is enough to say that if it is supposed that n ought to v, then any factor of the situation whose absence is incompatible with the truth of 'n ought to v' is one of the Facts, and any factor whose absence is compatible with the truth of 'n ought to v', but incompatible with the truth of ' 'n ought to v' and 'n v' ' belongs to the Circumstances. The application of this semantic principle presupposes a knowledge of the principles within each System which we rely on in our use of 'ought'. But since we have this knowledge (at least tacitly) we can learn about 'ought' by studying its use in various Systems.

An instructive place to start is with the use of 'ought' in generalizations in physical Systems.*

(67)   The most important evidence of traumatic shock is the victim's weakness coupled with a skin that is pale and moist and cooler than it ought to be.

An acceptable paraphrase of 67 could contain 'is normal' subbing for 'it ought to be'. It could not contain 'it has to be' or 'it would otherwise have to be' because factors other than traumatic shock might affect the skin temperature. 'Ought'

---

* In their instantiations the structure is the same, but strikes me as less evident.

seems specially suited for expressing this kind of generalization, which, to some, may seem an inferior brand, rough and ready, without the careful segregation of conditions required for a rigorous description of an invariable sequence in which 'must' or 'will' is employable. Inferior or not, we regularly describe the world in this manner, even in well-developed sciences. We—and it may be a little different for each one of us—have a general idea of how things proceed. Central to this idea is the conception of certain courses of events being natural or normal. Deviations from such a course of events are explained in terms of some intruding element. The absence of such elements constitutes what is often called 'normal circumstances', and, generally when 'ought' is used in contexts like 67, it also constitutes the Circumstances C.[2]

The preceding aids our understanding of 'ought' in moral contexts too. The use of 'ought', not 'must' or 'can', in a generalization is the most natural modal formulation of a moral law. In lieu of a (perhaps unattainable) detailing of exceptional circumstances which would permit the use of 'must', we say things like 'One ought not to steal.', thereby committing ourselves only to the claim that, in any particular case, either the theft was wrong or some excusing conditions exist. With 'ought' we avoid the dilemma of asserting either that theft is always and everywhere to be shunned (i.e., C continuously obtains because an adequate moral System admits no exceptional Circumstances for that act) or that it is never wrong (i.e., an adequate moral System contains no laws prohibiting theft).

Contrast this with the statements of the laws of legal and quasi-legal Systems: 'must' and 'can' are regularly used, but 'ought' rarely is. There the legislator cannot but achieve completeness when setting out the laws of the legal System just because the law is what the lawmaker says, and so any factor of a situation is relevant if and only if the lawmaker makes it so.* In short, the legislator is saying what must or can or must not or cannot be done. But when stating a moral law one is not (contra Kant) legislating: morally relevant considerations are not manufactured by proclamation. (I shall enlarge upon various aspects of all this later on.)

We should also note the curiosity that moral philosophers have so fixated on 'ought' and its synonyms that one can sift through shelves of books on morals without ever meeting 'can' or 'must' or its synonyms used in a moral context. This peculiar linguistic penchant demands explanation, since, if one listens to the actual speech of our linguistic community or reads fiction (I do not mean the philosophical variety), one discovers what is confirmed by the researches of M. Ehrman [3]—namely that 'can', 'must', and 'have (got) to' are each used in moral contexts about as much as 'ought' and 'shought' combined.† The source of the discrepancy between actual and philosophical usage is locatable in the definitions. 'Ought' differs from 'must' and the others in that to assert 'n ought to v' is not to assert that C obtains, and thus one can assert it with justification without an intimate knowledge of the surrounding Circumstances.‡ This makes 'ought' appropriate for the abstract, generalized sermonizings of phi-

---

* However, the application of the law may be problematic. It may be unclear whether I have broken the law 'n must not v', because it is unclear whether 'n v' correctly describes what I did. This may raise questions about the proper interpretation of the law, and about the meanings of 'n' and 'v'—but not about the meaning of 'must not'.

† This does not contradict the previous point about 'ought' in moral laws. One rarely says things like 'One ought not to steal.' except when addressing children—or unless one has the speech patterns of a prig. One rarely cites moral law in the midst of a serious moral argument. Or so it strikes me. Who does cite moral law? To whom? And when? The statistics would tell more about morality than any book of meta-ethics.

‡ But see pp. 124–125 concerning when one does have such knowledge.

losophers, theologians, and lesser moralists. And, contrariwise, 'must' and the others which require that C obtains are so commonly used in everyday speech just because everyday speech takes place within and is generally about concrete situations, detailed knowledge of which the speakers often have, or believe they have, or make it their business to acquire.

Not infrequently philosophers flatly misuse 'ought'; their illustrations of moral discourse and their moral pronouncements are linguistic grotesqueries because 'ought' is used where 'must' belongs or 'ought not' is used where 'must not' or 'cannot' belongs. (Occasionally they are moral grotesqueries as well, but for other reasons.) Surely the stentorian tones appropriate to the issuance of a Kantian verdict require 'must'; 'ought' simply won't bear the burden. And in general, anyone who conceives of a moral judgment as something like a command or imperative must have 'must', 'must not', and 'cannot' in mind, not 'ought' or 'ought not'. A judgment of the form 'n must v' entails a correlative judgment 'n v', and judgments of the form 'n must not v' and 'n cannot v' entail the correlative judgment '—(n v)'. Thus, given a relevant System such as a legal System, the utterance 'You must v' entails the imperative '(You) v!', and 'You cannot v' and 'You must not v' entail the imperative '—((You) v!)', that is, 'Don't v!'. (See pp. 139–140.) But 'n ought to v' does not entail the imperative 'v!'. To say 'You ought to do it.' is compatible with saying 'You don't have to do it.'; it is not even as strong as 'You must do it unless x' where x is some specific thing (e.g., you break your leg). To say 'You ought to do it.' is more like saying 'You must do it unless there is some reason not to do it.' (i.e., unless C does not obtain). And though '(You) do it unless there is some reason not to do it!' is an imperative,

The Meanings of the Modals

that only shows that not all imperatives can be used to tell someone what to do.

Given the right System, speaker, and situation, to say 'You ought to do it.' may be to advise or prescribe or the like. But though we do not speak of true or false advice or prescriptions, it does not follow that what is said in advising or prescribing (i.e., 'You ought to do it.') lacks a truth-value. On the contrary, the truth-value of what is said largely determines its value as advice or prescription. Indeed, unless the frame 'n ought to v' is embedded in an imperative or interrogative sentence, what is said when it is uttered always has a truth-value. Now, *some* illocutions (e.g., commands, prohibitions, permissions, laws) formed with indicative sentences are such that neither the illocution nor what is said can be assigned a truth-value. Two points about such illocutions. First, a mark of the successful production of such an illocution is that subsequent utterances of the same sentence can be true declarative illocutions: saying it makes it so. Second, they are often produced with 'n must (not) v' and 'n can(not) v', but never with 'n ought (not) to v'.

Where saying it makes it so, the declarative illocution is true in virtue of a prior utterance of the sentence being uttered by a speaker who is empowered by a System to produce the nondeclarative illocution in Circumstances consisting of the factors whose absence can cause the utterance to be what Austin calls "unhappy". Thus, if the President, a man empowered by his government to make promises for his government, says 'The United States promises to defend South Vietnam.', and the Circumstances are such that his utterance is not unhappy, then it is true that the United States promises to defend South Vietnam. Plugging these elements into the definitions of 'must', 'must not', 'can', and

119

'cannot' shows how saying a modal sentence can make what is said true. Suppose a city council says 'Dogs must be curbed.', and thereby enacts a law. The enactment has no truth-value, but subsequent utterances of that sentence can have a truth-value, for there exists an adequate relevant System, the city government, and a Fact about dogs, namely that the city council has said of them that they must be curbed. Furthermore, C obtains since the council successfully enacted the law. And finally, according to the city government, if the city council says 'Dogs must be curbed.' and C obtains, then it is illegal for a dog not to be curbed (i.e., 'n v' is true). This won't work with 'ought'. Since 'n ought to v' can be true even if C does not obtain, saying 'n ought to v' would make it true that n ought to v only if it didn't matter whether the non-declarative illocution had been successfully produced. That would be curious indeed.* Note further, even with 'must' and

---

* And yet, the English Bill of Rights of 1689 contains the sentence, "Excessive bail ought not to be required." However, this use of 'ought' does strike me as odd—not surprisingly, since the American Bill of Rights of 1791 contains the sentence "Excessive bail shall not be required." To my knowledge the legislative intent was the same, and this suggests some semantic shift. 'Ought' in contemporary legislation is most rare, and requires special situations. Section 132.390 of the current Oregon Revised Statutes reads: "The grand jury ought to find an indictment when all the evidence before it, taken together, is such as in its judgment would, if unexplained or uncontradicted, warrant a conviction by the trial jury." Given the special role of the grand jury (e.g., a jury that also can initiate investigation and prosecution and is often involved in the surveillance of local political matters) the intent and rationale of this section seem clear enough. While the grand jury is not bound ('must' or 'shall') to find an indictment in such cases, it is not simply empowered or permitted to do so. Nor should one say that it is left to the grand jury's discretion. Rather the grand jury is provisionally or presumptively bound: i.e., they will find an indictment in such cases, but if, in their judgment, there is some good reason for not doing so, they are permitted to refrain.

'can', saying it can't make it so if the relevant System is a moral code, because one can't make something into a morally relevant consideration by saying it is. Thus, with a moral System, what is said with 'n must (not) v', 'n can(not) v', or 'n ought (not) to v' *always* has a truth-value just as with a physical System. Well, *almost* always; in a moral System, as in many others, a few seemingly bona fide propositions may be bereft of truth-value for special reasons.

Now let us look at the use of 'ought' in formal Systems. We frequently say things like:

(68)   This proposition ought to be derivable from these five premises.

when it is plausible to suppose that 'n v' is true (that this proposition is derivable from these five premises), but we are unsure whether in fact it is true. Both in and out of formal Systems, sentences of the form 'n ought to v' are often so used. But in a formal System, once 'n v' is shown to be false, one cannot maintain that 'n ought to v' is true. It would make no clear sense to say

(69)   This proposition ought to be derivable from these five premises, but it isn't.

Nor would it help matters to add, 'Something must have gone wrong.'.* Now, formal Systems have two unique features: C always obtains,† and 'n ought to v' cannot be true

---

* The situation here must not be confused with one in which 'n v' is true (the proposition is derivable), but one has failed to prove it due to, for example, repeatedly making some miscalculation.

† I am not clear enough about the implications of Gödel's results to be able to say whether C may sometimes not obtain in a formal System. However, this really doesn't matter since this use of 'ought' does not presuppose mastery of Gödel's results.

if 'n v' is false. I submit that the former serves to explain the latter, and thereby explains the oddity of 69.

But this creates a puzzle as to how and why 'ought' is used in connection with formal Systems. Again, one might use a sentence like 68 when 'n v' seems true, but one is unsure. But though we use 'ought' in such situations, 'ought' never means that such a situation obtains.* The 'ought' of 68 means the same as elsewhere; it is still, so to speak, a provisional 'must'. That is, if n ought to v, then 'n v' is true—provided that C obtains. Thus 'ought' will commonly be used where one is unsure whether 'n v' is true because one has incomplete knowledge of the relevant factors.

Granted, in the context of a formal System one is not likely to be in doubt as to whether C obtains. But neither is one likely to be wondering whether the relevant System is adequate. Nor can we simply say that one is unsure whether some Fact about n is such that, according to the System, if the Fact and the Circumstances C obtain, then 'n v' is true. In a formal System the distinction between a Fact and the System is especially unclear,† since every true proposition 'Fn' is a law of the System (a rule or definition or theorem). Let me state the matter without the terminology of my account. One is probably unsure whether the application of certain rules on certain objects (numbers, sets, formulas, premises) will have such and such consequences. One is uncertain about the outcome of performing certain legitimate operations correctly. This is not the same as wondering

---

* Saying 'n ought to v' may conversationally implicate that such a situation obtains, but that is a separate issue from that of the meaning of the sentence.

† Later I discuss some general problems about the distinction between a Fact and a System (pp. 172–174).

whether C obtains—but it is similar. The term 'C' is designed to capture the idea that in applying the laws of a System, there may be room to wonder whether 'n v' is true. In a physical System, whether 'n v' is true depends on the details of the surrounding situation. In a formal System, whether 'n v' is true depends on the detailed working out of the legitimate operations. Let us not forget that there are *surprises* in mathematics and logic just as in the physical world. In both realms there is room for well-founded expectations which are defeated. With this much similarity it seems perfectly natural and appropriate that 'ought' should be used in both contexts.

It is time now to confront a consequence of my account that may have already sent my more logically astute readers scurrying for their red pencils. According to my definitions, 'n ought not to v' and 'n ought to v' are not genuine contraries. As one would expect, they can be simultaneously false, and, when C obtains, either one but not both may be true. But, when C does not obtain, they may be simultaneously true. I confess that, upon awakening to this result, I began to comfort myself with a fire made from the preceding pages. Then, having relieved my anguish, I rethought the matter and began rescuing the remnants. By now I can say (with only sporadic flinching) that it appears to be one of the most interesting and welcome results.

Let me begin to drain some of the paradox from this claim. First, recall (note, p. 110) that 'n ought not to v' is often used, not as the modal negation of 'n ought to v', but as the sentential negation: — (n ought to v). In the latter role it is a genuine contradictory of 'n ought to v' and the two cannot be simultaneously true (or simultaneously false). But whether a speaker means to be denying that n ought to v or affirming that v is something that n ought not to do is not always easily determined; sometimes the speech context contains insufficient clues, sometimes the speaker is not conscious of the difference, and this may cause confusion. On the other hand, if someone says 'n ought not to v' in response to someone else's utterance of 'n ought to v', his utterance will almost unavoidably be a denial of the prior utterance, that is, a sentential negation use—and this is an obstacle to displaying a conversation in which 'n ought to v' and 'n ought not to v' are simultaneously true.

Also, though less critical, the other ambiguity in 'ought not' mentioned earlier (note, p. 108), between negation of the modal itself and negation of the predicate, should be borne in mind. So actually we should distinguish affirming that v is something that n ought not to do, not only from denying that n ought to v, but also from affirming that —v is something that n ought to do.

There is another matter, one brought to my attention by John Cooper. We regard an utterance of 'n ought to v' (or 'n ought not to v') differently, depending on whether or not the speaker knew or believed that C does not obtain. (Sometimes it is enough that the speaker ought to have known, that, for example, he was or could easily have been in the position to know.) To repeat an earlier suggestion (see p. 122): ordinarily we use 'ought' where we think 'n v' is true but we aren't certain, and thus when we use it we conversationally implicate that such a situation obtains. We can cancel that implication by declaring our knowledge of the falsity of 'n v', but if we have that knowledge and don't declare it, then our utterance will be criticizable in various ways and degrees depending upon the context of utterance. For instance,

The Meanings of the Modals

I may say, 'I agree that you ought to stand behind a man who has been so good to you, but you ought not to, you must not keep silent about what he has done, no matter what the consequences may be for him.'.* If in the situation that prompts that speech I were to say instead simply 'You ought to stand behind a man who has been so good to you.', my remark would be, at the very least, misleading and irresponsible. So, it can be quite objectionable and quite wrong to *say* 'n ought to v' (or 'n ought not to v') when C does not obtain, but it may still be true.

Next recall that, purely on the basis of linguistic intuitions, we would place 'ought' somewhere between 'must' and 'may' (where 'may' is not replaceable by 'can'). So compare:

(69)   He must do it, and then again he must not.

(70)   He may do it, and then again he may not.

(71)   He ought to do it, and then again he ought not.

Sentence 69 is clearly unacceptable; 'must' and 'must not' are undeniably contraries. With an SI, 70 is also unacceptable, but with an SA it is not, because there 'may' and 'may not' are not contraries at all.† And now, I hope my reader senses

---

* The falsity of the 'C obtains' component in the protasis of the hypothetical mmm of an 'n ought to v' assertion does not falsify that assertion. But the features of the situation which falsify 'C obtains' can also be considered Facts, which, when taken in conjunction with the rest of the situation, imply that '— (n v)' is true, thereby supporting the correlative 'n ought not v' assertion and the stronger claims, 'n must not v' and 'n cannot v'.

† As an added fillup, I suggest the following as a way of incorporating a definition of 'may' into my general account of the modals. In essence 'n may v' has the same definition as 'n can v' plus an indicator that there is some likelihood (probability) that 'n v' is true. This works when the relevant System is an SA. And since there is no room for the notion of probability or likelihood in SI's, the likelihood indicator becomes void

as I do that, while 71 is not as obviously acceptable as 70, it is not as unacceptable as 69 either. (Perhaps it would sound better if fitted into a context such as: 'Well Charlie, you know how it is. It's one of those crazy situations . . . ') This is how it should be, since 'ought' requires special circumstances for its noncontrariety with 'ought not' to appear. Again, everything is as one would expect when C obtains; 'ought' and 'ought not' behave like genuine contraries. Things are not what one would expect only when C does not obtain—and that is just what one ought to expect! That is, when the Circumstances are such that the laws of the relevant System do not accurately determine whether 'n v' is true, one can anticipate that surprise and confusion will be consequences and that one may not know quite what to say. To see this, let us put aside definitions and preconceptions, and test our linguistic intuitions on a particular case.

Here is an example. Again, to make it sound all right it helps to suppose that the two speakers are coincidentally, not conversationally, speaking about the same subject.

(72)   Flora: I just don't understand it. Two hours ago I put a five pound roast in the oven at 350°. I just checked it. The oven is working fine, but the roast is practically raw. I can't imagine what went wrong, but something must have, because the roast certainly ought to be done by now.

(73)   Mildred: Well, there is no getting around it. The roast ought not to be done for another hour now. I found out from Chrissy that the children—those

when the relevant System is an SI, thereby leaving 'n may v' equivalent to 'n can v'. That is, because the laws of an SI are not based on the regularities of actual events, one cannot talk about the probability of 'n v' being true in an SI, and thus 'may' reduces to 'can'.

little scamps—were playing in the kitchen and turned off the oven because the room was so hot, and they didn't turn it back on till they left.

Now, need we suppose that either Flora or Mildred is mistaken about something they said? I am not asking whether they are justified in saying what they said, for there should be no doubt about that; I am asking whether either of them has said anything false. In view of the total situation evidently the roast *won't* be done for another hour, but at this juncture it should be beyond cavil that '—(n v)' does not entail '—(n ought to v)'. Still, it may be granted that if either of them is mistaken, Flora is when she says 'the roast certainly ought to be done by now'. After all, Mildred can make the even stronger claim that the roast couldn't be done by now. And wouldn't Flora retract her claim if she knew what Mildred knows?—But would she? Need she? Couldn't she reply, 'Nonetheless, it ought to be done by now.' (or perhaps, 'Nonetheless, it ought to have been done by now.')? Would she be linguistically deviant if she said that? Is that even false? To these questions I would answer that Flora isn't and wasn't mistaken, and that what she did say and might reply are not false. However, it should be added that if you were to ask me these questions in an ordinary situation I might start feeling somewhat cowed and defensive. I might simply describe the situation, including the fact that the roast won't be done for another hour, for I would want to know what of any importance really turns on whether I— or we—say in such a case 'n ought to v'. ("Say what you choose, so long as it does not prevent you from seeing the facts. ([And when you see them there is a good deal you will not say.]" [4])

The Significance of Sense

This last point might be parried by picking a case with a moral issue at stake. Here, so it might be thought, it certainly does matter what we say. But that is not quite true. What matters is what we do; what we say is of consequence primarily in the ways in which it is bound up with what we do.

Apt moral examples are plentiful. The real question is what they are examples of: i.e., is my account the proper explanation of the phenomena? The answer my reader gives is some measure of the extent to which he is emancipated from the idea that saying 'You ought to v' is a convoluted way of telling you to v. Recall now the earlier discussion of 'ought' in moral laws (pp. 116–117). Left out there is the fact that, although we regularly say things like 'One ought not to steal.', 'One ought to help those in need.', we still feel some discomfort about it. We feel like saying that, yes, that's true—but yet it's not really true because what if you must steal to save your starving mother, or if . . . , or if . . . . So we may try to amend the original assertion by tacking on a long list of exceptions. But it turns out—or so it seems— that the list is uncompletable. And then perhaps we feel that there are no moral principles. (What goes unnoticed is that if the list were completed the assertion would still be odd, for then 'must', 'must not', or 'cannot' would be the proper expression.) I submit that our initial instincts are right. It is true that one ought not to steal and true that in some cases one ought to steal. There is no contradiction here, but 'ought' is so structured that it is altogether natural to feel that there is one. And I further submit that the ambivalence we feel in such cases, both moral and nonmoral, is a leading linguistic fact about 'ought'. A significant virtue of my account is that an explanation of that fact is provided.

The Meanings of the Modals

Another unexpected upshot of the unasserted 'C obtains' is that, although 'must' entails 'ought,' and 'must not' and 'cannot' entail 'ought not', 'ought' is compatible with 'must not' and 'cannot', and 'ought not' is compatible with 'must'. Again, this is less paradoxical than first appears. After all, it is in keeping with our intuitions that, whereas 'must' is incompatible with 'may (might) not', 'ought' is not, and that, whereas 'must not' and 'cannot' are incompatible with 'may (might)', 'ought not' is not. More directly, since 'must not' and 'cannot' entail the falsity of 'n v' and 'ought' does not entail its truth, they are stronger than and overrule 'ought', and since 'must' entails the truth of 'n v' and 'ought not' does not entail its falsity, 'must' is stronger than and overrules 'ought not'. In consequence certain sentences are odd, and some are odder than others. Compare:

(46)   You cannot see him, but you ought to.
(74)   You ought to see him, but you cannot.

Though 74 sounds somewhat odd (especially when detached from any context), it is not as odd as 46. Neither sentence expresses a self-contradiction, and, as far as sentence meaning goes, they are interchangeable. However, word order is controlled not just by semantic and syntactic rules, but also, according to Grice's theory, by general rules of conversation. Compare:

(75)   I fried the eggs and ate them.
(76)   I ate the eggs and fried them.

The structure of 76 is odd, not because of the meaning of 'and', but because, when we describe a series of events, generally we mention them in the order that they occurred. Now compare:

(77)   It might happen and it ought to.
(78)   It ought to happen and it might.

Sentence 77 is quite acceptable, but 78 is unnatural because 'ought' is stronger than 'might', so that, once it is said that it ought to happen, it seems pointless to add that it might. Similarly, 46 sounds odder than 74, because, once one says 'cannot', 'ought' is already overridden, so the belated 'ought' seems a pointless afterthought.

As a final bit of corroboration for my account I want to say a little about the etymology of 'ought'. What I shall say is too suppositious to bear much probative force. Still, I think the fact that 'ought' and its synonym 'shought' have independent genealogies, yet derive from preterite verbs meaning 'to owe' indicates that the etymology will be instructive.

In her article, "Brute Facts", Anscombe presents an analysis of 'owe'. As she hints there and states more explicitly in a companion piece,[5] she chose this word because of its etymological relation to 'ought'. She frames her analysis as an answer to the question behind the naturalistic fallacy: how can one derive a proposition of the form 'b owes c' from a set of propositions describing the facts of a situation? Her answer is not merely compatible with my account of 'ought'; it coincides with my account.* In essence, she says that the use of 'owe presupposes a particular institution (read: System), but in no way describes or mentions or refers to it. (Read: the definition of 'ought' does not contain a reference to or description of any System.) To establish the assertion 'b owes

---

* It is no coincidence that it does. Her article was one source of inspiration for my account, and thus is not an independent verification of my hypothesis. Nonetheless, it is striking that our analyses of 'ought' and 'owe' reveal similar fundamental structures.

The Meanings of the Modals

c' within the context of that institution, one need only cite certain facts (read: Facts) which are brute relative to the fact that b owes c. (Read: according to the System y there is a law '$(x)(Fx \supset Vx)$'.) If these facts obtain (read: 'Fn' is true) and if the surrounding circumstances are normal (read: C obtains), then it follows that b owes c (read: 'n ought to v'). There is no need to carry the analogy further; obviously it will break down eventually. After all, 'ought' no longer means 'owe.'

But Anscombe's analysis does not take us far enough. It was intended as an analysis applicable to large numbers of "descriptive" terms, not just to 'owe'. So one is left wondering about the special features of 'owe' which gave birth to 'ought' and 'shought'. So now I want to offer an hypothesis. First, without conceding that 'ought' is now used specially in moral contexts, we can grant that it may once have been so used. Next I offer the quite unoriginal idea that many of our moral concepts are shaped by our legal and economic history, and that many of the central terms of our moral vocabulary (e.g., 'duty') have their origin in the intercourse between law and business, especially contract law. Thus, it should not be surprising if the word that is now thought of as the focal point of a moral judgment—'ought'—derives from the word that serves as the focus of interest in contractual relations—'owe'. We might say that 'owe', the word that signals the conclusion of bargaining, became 'ought', the word that signals the conclusion of a moral argument. This hypothesis seems buttressed by the fact that within the System of rules of commerce, 'b owes c' is virtually synonymous with 'b ought to c'. More precisely, within that System, once it is settled that b (a person) owes c (a sum or service) to d (a person), there is no further, additional question whether b ought to v (pay or perform c to (or for) d). So, 'ought', having inherited the role and logical structure of 'owe', began, to move into the context of a moral System. It was not much of a trip, since then, even more than now (if that is possible), law, business, and morality merged and mingled in a variety of ways. The next step, the transference to the context of other kinds of Systems, becomes readily understandable through the work of Piaget and others. (See pp. 141–148) Some time before the Renaissance, when these transformations were occurring, the various kinds of Systems were not as conceptually distinct as they now are. Thus, one imagines, it would be natural to move 'ought' into kinds of Systems that later became more fully distinguished from the moral and quasi-moral Systems in which it originated.

Again, this proves nothing. It is intended to be merely suggestive. It ought to help make clear how we could come to have such a curious word as 'ought'.

Joseph Margolis has recently argued for the univocity of 'ought'. Since his account is univocalist, he can and does draw many of the same conclusions as I do, and thus I have little philosophical incentive for warring with him. Still, a synopsis of some defects of his account helps to clarify the structure and motivations behind mine. My criticisms, however, are tentative, for, at crucial points, Margolis speaks in a vague or loose manner—enough so that his account might be read as a sketchy version of what I have tried to express.

Margolis' account employs the sense-criteria distinction used by others to define 'good' and similar words. Margolis writes:

Respecting its sense, I suggest that 'ought' has the force of a predicate expression rather than of a verb or auxiliary verb. It is used to characterize some item as superior or first in rank or preference or the like among a set of relevant alternatives, in some respect to be supplied in context; the respect in which such ordering obtains governs the relevant criteria of appraisal.[6]

Apparently, Margolis treats 'ought' as a predicate because he supposes that a "modal interpretation characteristically presupposes the doctrine of ' "ought" implies "can" ' " [7]—a doctrine which we agree is false and my modal account shows to be such. That aside, the treatment of 'ought' (and presumably 'should' which he never mentions) as a predicate is utterly unmotivated, while sitting squarely against every syntactical consideration. But then, Margolis leaves unexplained the point or force of saying that 'ought' "has the force of a predicate expression." Assuredly, one could rig up a predicate correlated to 'ought', and transform sentences with 'ought' on the model of the transformations of sentences with 'must' and 'can' into sentences with 'necessary' and 'possible'. Apparently this is what Margolis has in mind, since, on the basis of his sample of paraphrases, I assume he takes n v to be the "item" that 'ought' is "used to characterize." So, 'ought' can be treated as a predicate—just as every modal auxiliary verb can (and as 'precedes' can be treated as a preposition). Of course, some problems attend this move. It is tantamount to denying the existence of the modal auxiliary verbs as a distinct syntactic class. And if 'ought', 'must', and the rest were predicates they would be eligible for an appearance in the consequent of contrary-to-fact conditionals, but they aren't. And if they were predicates, 'n *mod. aux.* not v' would always be equivalent to '—(n *mod. aux.* v)', but it isn't. And so on. However, the weight of such objections is not to be measured without determining what is at stake in Margolis' elision of matters of syntax.

Independently of syntax, the semantics of his account is worrisome. The phrase "superior or first in rank or preference or the like" strongly suggests that Margolis is defining 'ought' in terms of 'good'. His sample paraphrases with their repeated use of variants of 'would be the best X' tend to confirm this hypothesis. (At the same time, the appearance of 'would' seems to belie the predicative, nonmodal nature of the definition.) Such a definition seems suspect on several grounds. Many philosophers might deem it an unenlightening, however accurate, definition. Others might balk at the potential defense by definition of consequentialism. Another drawback is the hash this account makes of 'ought''s etymology, for the definiens does not connect with anything in the word's history. Also, I would question whether the definition permits a distinction between 'ought' and 'must', since it fits 'must' at least as well and perhaps better than 'ought'. Allied with this point, a sentence like 'The roast ought to be done by now, but it isn't.' has an air of paradox on a Margolian reading: That the roast is done is the likeliest estimate of its present condition, but it isn't done. More. We get no hint of why words like 'absolutely' sit uneasily with 'ought', and why 'ought' is naturally used with some Systems (moral, physical), but not others (legal, games). And so on. In a word, Margolis' account neglects the provisional aspect of 'ought'. Finally, 'ought' would presumably be a syncategorematic predicate like 'good'. So, the multiple illocutionary and propositional potential of sentences with 'ought' should be due to a sentence incompleteness remediable by supplying an appropriate noun phrase—but it isn't. The unclarity of an utterance with 'ought' is cobbled, not by precise specification of the relevant category of objects (as with 'good'), but by specifying a relevant System of laws (reasons). If 'ought' sentences are incomplete, what they lack is an elaborate explanatory clause: n ought to v, because . . . . And, anyway, there is no reason to think 'ought' sentences are incomplete.

Four

The Modals and Morality

> To primitive man [and children], the moral and the
> physical universe are one and the same thing, and a rule
> is both a law of nature and a principle of conduct.
> —Jean Piaget, *The Moral Judgment of the Child*

THE fundamentals of my account have been presented, but
various aspects of it may yet be puzzling or unconvincing, so
more needs to be said. This chapter has the function, and
hence the form, of a mop-up operation. An odd lot of topics
are casually arranged under three main subjects: the interrelations of SI's, the relations of SI's to SA's, the naturalistic
fallacy. The size of the discussions increases in that order.
What I shall say herein does not solve any philosophical
problems; at best it may serve to identify a few.

The multiple propositional potential of modal sentences can
cause confusion. It may be true according to my nation's
legal System that I must bomb Vietnamese peasants while it
is true according to an adequate moral System that I must
not bomb Vietnamese peasants (and thus, false that I must
do it). However, an adequate moral System can undermine

the legal claim by denying that the legal System is adequate (legitimate): i.e., the j of the 'n must v' legal proposition is false. That is, I take it that one requirement of an adequate moral System is that it state some requirements of an adequate legal System. (The problems of political obligation and legitimate revolution enter here.) Though these restrictions limit the amount of conflict between the judgments based on the two Systems, I doubt that the restrictions would suffice to preclude all such conflict. At this juncture we face the problems of civil disobedience. Sometimes the State's claim can still be undermined, for example, by showing the relevant laws to be unconstitutional, and thus not valid laws (i.e., jjj is false). But sometimes this tactic is not available.

At this stage various wrong moves are tempting. One might say, "My country right or wrong, my country!", thereby espousing a moral System pre-empting conflict between morality and legality. Such a moral System is not self-contradictory, but it is inadequate. Or one might declare that if the State says I must do something which an adequate moral System says I must not do, then what the State says is false. This position presupposes that a legal System is adequate only if what it says does not *ever* oppose what is said by an adequate moral System—and that is, I think, an unrealistic requirement. Or one might say that the utterances of the State have no truth-value at all, for they are statutes, decrees, verdicts, and so forth. This is true, but in virtue of those statutes and the like certain propositions about what the citizens must do are true.

The proposition '(Legally) I must bomb Vietnamese peasants.' may be true while the proposition '(Morally) I must bomb Vietnamese peasants.' is false. These are different propositions whose truth-values may differ because the Systems referred to are of different kinds. There is a conflict here, but no contradiction. Within the domain of the legal System it is true that I must do it, and if I don't I thereby do something wrong (illegal). The extralegal considerations of morality are, by definition, irrelevant. Equally, it is irrelevant to the moral claim that the proposition based on an unjust law is true; unless I violate the statute I do something wrong (immoral). The conflict is not between two propositions, but between two (partly) independent Systems. The real problem is not which proposition is true, but which System I am to act in accord with. And since, I take it, in general the reason for obeying a legal System is based on a moral System (and/or a System of maximizing utility),* one may lack a reason to obey when the act is immoral. This is a problem for an adequate moral System. Perhaps sometimes it would direct one to violate the law *and* accept the legal consequences. Note, although one may try to alter the legal System, even if successful one does not alter the truth-value of propositions based on the legal System; rather one makes it come to be that certain utterances are no longer utterances of true propositions.†

---

* A System of maximizing utility describes the behavior of an optimally rational agent with certain desires, information, and opportunities who is seeking to maximize the satisfaction of his system of desires. It differs from an adequate moral System by giving no weight to the desires of others which have no effect on the satisfaction of the agent's desires.

† A related though separate problem is that of the possible conflict of propositions based on an adequate moral System and an adequate System of maximizing utility. In essence this is the problem of why one should (or is it must?) be moral. I would like to have a nice solution to this problem. I do not, largely because I am unsure of what the problem is. I do not think it is a spurious problem (though no doubt some versions of it are). I feel more certain that the attempts to show it to be spurious rest on specious arguments than I am that it is spurious. I think it

The judgments based on an SA do not conflict in this way with those based on an SI, and this may make my reader suspicious. Intuitively, if any distinction marks an ambiguity in the modals, it would be the SA-SI distinction. And matters may seem worsened rather than helped by my treatment of the laws of an SI and the nonmodal sentence 'n v'. It may seem *ad hoc*, sophistical, indefensible, and my account's need of it may only reflect badly on the account.

When I introduced these matters (pp. 89–92) I appealed to accepted usage and gave one example from a quasi-legal text. Other evidence is available. Keep in mind that the Systems qualifying as SI's include not only moral codes, codes of etiquette, legal systems, and games, but, equally, languages, logic, and mathematics. Within the context of descriptive linguistics, the sentence 'The first letter of the first word of a written English sentence is capitalized.' would be a generalization describing a regularity, but it is more naturally used and taken as the statement of a rule. If I write a sentence and violate that rule, I do not falsify what is said in uttering that sentence; rather, I thereby do something wrong. No ambiguity is at work here. The sentence 'If seven is added to fifteen, the result is twenty-two.' is most naturally used and interpreted so that what is said is not falsified by the fact that frequently when seven is added to fifteen the result is twenty-three or twenty-one. Granted, one clarifies what is meant when uttering that sentence by using either 'If seven is *correctly* added to fifteen, the result is twenty-two.' or 'If seven is added to fifteen, the *correct* result is twenty-two.', but

---

is simply false that self-interest and morality never conflict. And I see no way of solving the problem by appealing to the meanings of 'ought' or 'moral'. Part of the puzzle is that it is unclear what would be the relevant System supporting the proposition 'One ought to be moral.'.

138

this only sharpens my point, for neither of these latter sentences is synonymous with the first. Even when solidly within a moral context this point holds good; I may say 'We (or You) don't shoot a man for trespassing.' precisely because you did.

Still, though this points to literally countless numbers of sentences having this dual use, one might insist that they form a special class. So let us go a step further. A System enters into speech primarily in the form of reasons for what we say. Thus its primary effect should be upon illocutionary force, not upon word or sentence meaning. And since the SA-SI distinction corresponds roughly (not exactly!) to the theoretical-practical distinction, it is to be expected that it will parallel roughly (not exactly!) the distinction between declarative and practical illocutions. This expectation is met. Sentences like 'It stays there.', 'It is staying there.', 'It will stay there.', are supremely ordinary, yet they are used not only in declarative illocutions but also in commands, orders, and the like. The speaker can say that p is the case or command that it be the case that p. If 'p' is false, then so is what the speaker said in the first case, but not in the second—instead, in his eyes, someone has done something wrong. No ambiguity need be involved here. No doubt it is tempting to construe such sentences in the latter use as ellipses of imperative sentences like 'Make sure that it stays there!'. But there is no more to recommend that move than a move to treat the imperative sentence as an ellipsis for an indicative sentence like 'I order you to make sure that it stays there.'.

This last suggestion was facetious, but I do have a serious one to offer regarding the imperative mood. First, let me grant that some semantic and syntactic devices indicate whether the relevant System is an SA or an SI—if there weren't, we would have no way of saying which System is relevant. One such device is the imperative mood. Different languages form the imperative mood in different ways, but the details do not matter here. Earlier (pp. 118–119) I stated that, given the right kind of System, 'n must v' can entail 'v!', and 'n must not v' and 'n cannot v' can entail '—v!' (Don't v!'). Implicit there was the suggestion that imperative sentences can be treated as indicative sentences with indicators (e.g., subject deletion) that the relevant System is to be an SI. The advantages of so construing the imperative mood are manifold. For one thing, it seems altogether natural for the utterance of second person present and future tense indicative sentences connected to an SI to be practical illocutions such as commands, orders, imperatives, or directives. Further, one can understand the illocutionary force of an utterance of an imperative sentence by associating the indicative counterpart with the appropriate SI. For example, '(You) add five and carry the remainder.' would be an instruction if the System were a mathematical one; a warning, threat, or advice if the System were a System of maximizing utility; a command if the System were a quasi-legal System (e.g., teacher ordering pupil). If you don't add five and carry the remainder then you have done something wrong, but the respect in which it is wrong depends on the relevant System. Furthermore, this analysis offers an elegant logical calculus for the imperative mood, namely the same one used for the indicative mood. A new logic replete with synthetic plastic phrastics and similar gimcrackery is unnecessary. If the imperative sentence is used to express a proposition in an SI, we can apply the normal calculus to these propositions.

But such matters are of secondary importance, because it is not a semantic question whether a System is an SA or an

The Modals and Morality

SI. Whether a *specific* System is one or the other is a question of fact about how the people who use the System treat its laws. And whether an *adequate* System of a certain *kind* is an SA or an SI is settled not by semantics but by Theory construction. The language (i.e., the vocabulary and grammar) of a System need not expose it as an SA or an SI; what makes it one or the other is the way the laws are treated. If in general a counterinstance to a law is treated as a reason for criticizing the law, then the System is an SA. And if in general a counterinstance to a law is treated as a reason for criticizing the violation, then the System is an SI. Roughly, a law of an SA is a description of a regularity, and a law of an SI is a norm (which is not to say that it must lack a truth-value). This is a difference in illocutionary force, and thus in the use of sentences, not necessarily in their meaning or grammatical form. It is a further separate question how the laws of a certain *kind* of System *should* be treated. This is determined on grounds internal to the problem of the requirements of an adequate System of that kind. To make this vivid, it helps to see that *in fact* not all physical Systems are SA's and not all moral Systems are SI's.

The work of Jean Piaget and his successors indicates that human intellectual development proceeds according to an invariable pattern of sequential stages. From infancy to intellectual maturity a human being's conception of his universe —logical, physical, and moral—undergoes a series of radical transformations. What we as adults take for granted as a rational and coherent conceptual scheme is not what we had as children. And, as the researches of cultural anthropologists into the mentality of primitive peoples reveal, neither is our conceptual scheme possessed by even the adults of primitive societies.

The Significance of Sense

Much of Piaget's theory is still highly controversial, and some of it has, in my judgment, been subject to devastating criticism, most notably in the field of moral development by Lawrence Kohlberg. But, to my knowledge, the elements of his theory to which I appeal have withstood criticism and are receiving increasingly widespread endorsement.

Piaget maintains that our (adult) conceptual scheme differs from children's and primitives' not merely in content, but even in the conceptual *structures* with which the world is understood. The situation is misdescribed by saying that they (children and primitives) are simply ignorant or misinformed about certain facts, thereby assimilating the case to one in which we are ignorant of misinformed. The disparities are not exemplified by the differences between a fitteenth-century European scientist who thought the earth was flat and a twentieth-century scientist who believes the earth is an oblate spheroid. Nor, in the realm of morals, is the difference that they believe things to be right (e.g., stealing) which we believe to be wrong, for, by and large, unanimity exists on that level. The divergencies are more akin to those separating us from the paranoid schizophrenic in Georgia who thought an international conspiracy sought to capture his testes, which were made of radium. Like a schizophrenic, a normal child has a profoundly different conception both of what the brute facts are and of how they relate to other facts. The very structure of the relation between evidence and conclusion is different.*

---

* It is neither prudent nor necessary for my purposes to press very hard the analogies between infant, primitive, and aberrant mentalities, as Blondel and psychoanalytic theorists have. After all, as Lévi-Strauss nicely points out, "not only are there children, primitives and lunatics, but also primitive children and primitive lunatics, and both primitive and civilized psychopathic children." [1]

The Modals and Morality

Our intellectual development does not consist of the accumulation of data imprinted upon a *tabula rasa*. Nor are we born with a set of fixed concepts that persist into adulthood. And neither do we have even the same fundamental conceptual structure lasting throughout our lives. Instead, we pass through a number of distinguishable stages which are marked by distinct conceptions of space, time, causality, number, justice, conservation, law, and other fundamental notions. The raw data of perception (if there be such things) are processed, organized, and understood differently at each stage. Put in my terminology, at each stage we have fundamentally different moral, physical, and logical Systems.

The aspect of this conceptual development which most immediately concerns my account is presented in the following passage from Piaget.

To primitive man, the moral and physical universe are one and the same thing, and a rule is both a law of nature and a principle of conduct. For this very reason, a crime threatens the very existence of the universe and must be mystically set at naught by a suitable expiation. But this idea of a law that is both physical and moral is the very core of the child's conception of the world; for under the effect of adult constraint the child cannot conceive the laws of the physical universe except in the guise of a certain obedience rendered by things to rules.[2]

Piaget calls this stage 'realism'; we might call it actualism. An essential characteristic of this stage is the belief in immanent justice. This is the belief (actually, it is or involves a whole system of beliefs) that *in fact* the world is so constituted that *it* unfailingly punishes violators of the laws and rewards those who are obedient. Coupled with and sustaining this is the conception of natural laws and the behavior of physical objects in terms of the manipulations of an agent.

Put it this way: the sentence 'A man is punished if and only if he violates some law.' could be used to express a law in either an SA or an SI. In the child's conceptual scheme it does both. And because he conceives the world in animistic terms, he can take certain events to be punishments which we cannot so take.

Thus we find that *in fact* the moral System of children and primitives is classifiable as an SA and their physical System as an SI. Or, to be more accurate, it can be said that the infantile conceptual scheme admits no clear distinction between an SA and an SI. At minimum it must be conceded that a quite commonly held moral System is not neatly classifiable as an SI and a quite commonly held physical System is not neatly classifiable as an SA. And, as I shall later argue, a genuine intellectual achievement in Theory construction, not a wholesale alteration of his dictionary, is required for man, both ontogenetically and phylogenetically, to abandon the notions of immanent justice and other notions peculiar to the stage of realism.

Since some of my readers may lack easy access to a child or a primitive man, they may have qualms about these empirical claims. But the phenomena are visible in various quarters; one need only know what to look for. Not every "normal" adult of civilized societies attains the higher levels of Theory development. It is common for vestiges of one's infantile beliefs to persist into adulthood, sometimes coexisting uncomfortably with more developed conceptions.

Look at the Book of Job. It can be read as a story of intellectual crisis. Job has attained an intellectual stage in advance of his interlocutors who show themselves incapable of fully understanding and accepting the idea that misfortune could befall a man who has been obedient to the law. Since

144

it is undeniable that Job is suffering, the inescapable conclusion for them is that he is not innocent—he *must* somehow have violated the law. Job is beyond that stage; he is able to perceive and accept the fact that he is both suffering and innocent. He is thus forced to abandon the notion of the reality of immanent justice. Yet this leaves him in a conceptual quandary, for he still conceives of the natural and moral order as controlled by an omnipotent moral being, a Father-figure. Thus, the problem of evil. It is a genuine problem for anyone at this juncture in his intellectual development. Job deals with it in the only way one can at that stage: he submissively accepts God's word when He gives, in effect, the excuse given by despotic parents to their children since time beyond history—'You're too young to understand.'. Awed by God's power and knowledge, conscious of his complete inferiority and dependence, lacking any critical tools except those that the Parent has provided, Job is without defense; there can be no argument.*

Ultimately the problem is solved in only one way—you make the intellectual leap made by Laplace; you develop a System in which the postulation of an agent is not required for an adequate explanation of the physical universe. But even that achievement, profound as it is, is not sufficient, for you are left a Kirilov: the parent is gone and with him the parental constraints. Nietzsche rightly saw this as a stage of cultural crisis posing an array of alternatives. Do you stay in this state and remain a confused and corrupted child? Or do you accept the unreality of the law and become a nihilist?

---

* It is worth remembering in this connection that the Moral Law was delivered and understood as a set of *command*ments. This is, of necessity, the child's first conception of morality. For the benighted, it is their only conception.

Or do you take the further step of constructing a new moral System and become a man?

Admittedly this scrap of ontogenetic-phylogenetic history is too impressionistic to be probative. Still, it may give my reader an inkling of the kind of transformation I am talking about, and it dramatizes how a moral System could be an SA, and thus how a violation of a moral law could lead one to reject the law and perhaps the whole of morality.

Further evidence for the developmental thesis is derivable from the works of famous philosophers. However, such material is suspect as illustration, let alone evidence, without a full-scale digression on the developmental thesis and some philosophical theories.* Still it seems fair to asseverate that the philosophy of science espoused by Plato has more affinity with the physical Systems of primitive man than with those of contemporary scientists. An equally fair, though more con-

---

* Yet, alas, even an independent volume on the subject is likely to be without effect. As Dewey noted, philosophers are loth to have their cerebrations explained in sociopsychological terms. (Unhappily, due to their tendency to explain the philosophical theory *away*, most of the attempts in this direction are worthy of their dismissive reception.) This is especially true when any philosopher of historical repute is the target, for we are all, to one extent or another, their epigones. And the hoarier the tradition, the more sympathetically and the less justly we read and assess. But perhaps to regard this as cause for complaint is only to exhibit a misconception of the subject; the history of philosophy seems more akin to the history of art than to the history of science.

Ethics (where, if any place, biography could not be irrelevant to philosophy) is haunted by its own brand of professional courtesy. Academic moral philosophers seem disinclined to let the moral beliefs of a colleague have a bearing on his professional stature. (This is, I take it, both a cause and a consequence of the dominance of meta-ethics.) So ingrained is this habit that its singularity goes unnoticed. Imagine the reception which philosophers of science would award a colleague who espoused the phlogiston theory!

tentious, claim would be that Kant's moral philosophy is a defense of a somewhat primitive moral System decked out in metaphysical trappings. Taking Kant's writings all in all, as he surely wanted them to be taken, he ranks as a virtual paradigm of a stage 4 personality in Kohlberg's theory of moral development. (The highest stage is 6; my ten-year-old is at stage 3, edging toward 4.) This is an empirical claim, not a value judgment, but without a careful presentation of Kohlberg's and Kant's theories I would make no pretense of proving it.* Even without such proof I am disposed to regard the received opinion that Kant is the greatest modern moral philosopher as an uncompromising indictment of a whole genre.†

I admit (if admission be called for) that my last remark is

---

* Admittedly, Kohlberg takes Kant to be expressing a stage 6 System, but he has read only the *Foundations*, and thus, I believe, has misread it. (Not so Piaget: "in Kant's personal mentality there are many traces of heteronomy and legalism." [3]) For instance, both a stage 4 and a stage 6 personality would say that a man must be treated as an end, never as a means only, but for Kant, though not for a stage 6 personality, that is compatible with unmitigated subservience to the state, the *lex talionis*, and other practices of varying degrees of wickedness. (Cf. Nietzsche: "Kant, whose categorical imperitive smacks of cruelty." [4])

† It will be said that, while Kant's moral beliefs may be an embarrassment, his contributions to "analytical" moral philosophy are substantial. That dichotomy is unrealistic in fact, if not in principle, for stage differences are marked not so much by the moral verdicts as by the kinds of arguments used. Key sections of the *Foundations* bewilder sophisticated commentators, but the problems and paradoxes are hidden from the eyes of a stage 4 personality. For example, critics justly complain that the universalizability criterion is empty since the outcome of its application depends on the maxim used and hence on the description of the situation. Yet, for a stage 4 personality the description of a situation is umproblematic: e.g., "It's a lie."; special circumstances, motives, and consequences don't enter into it. (See Kant's, "On a Supposed Right to Tell Lies from Benevolent Motives.")

a value judgment; so too is the modern chemist's claim that the phlogiston theory is no longer worth considering. I am not, however, committing the genetic or evolutionary fallacies (if they be fallacies). I am not assaying Systems on the basis of their birth dates, ontogenetic or phylogenetic. After all, Plato postdated the Greek Atomists. The historical sequence is a prima facie consideration, but not sufficient evidence. Systems are not superannuated. But, first, the developmental theorists are not talking about a random chronological order; they are concerned with a regular, replicatable progression explicable by reference to the greater rationality of each later System over every earlier one. Second, Piaget and Kohlberg do not pretend to justify the later Systems; they merely assume, as any sane scientist must, that their conception of reality is superior to those of primitive people and children, that the Systems educated adults consider the best available are superior to those they have rejected. But they explicitly treat the question of whether any fundamental conception of moral or physical reality is "better" than any other as a philosophical one.[5] They are quite right; that is a genuine philosophical problem, and it is solved, not by high-level lexicography, but by an investigation into the requirements of adequate Systems.

Even at this late point, my insistence on involving a System in every use of a modal might be thought unwarranted, since, supposedly, in numerous simple situations a modal can be used unsupported by appeal to some System. For example, I try and fail to push a pissoir off a piazza, and then say:

(1)   I can't budge it.

Or better still, to avoid some red herrings, suppose I say:

(2)   I couldn't budge it then.

The Modals and Morality

The simplicity of the situation is only apparent. We start with two Facts: I tried to budge it, and I failed to budge it. And I am contending that without an adequate relevant System that is all I could justifiably assert. For these two Facts certainly don't entail 2,* so how is this 'can' derived from this 'is'?

One might paraphrase 2 in either of two ways:

(2E)   Even if certain facts had been different (e.g., the pavement had not been so slippery), it would not have been budged by me.

(2U)   Unless certain facts had been different, it would not have been budged by me.

On either interpretation one would be appealing to the common-sense Theory one has about the response of physical objects to certain amounts of force. Clearly 2E rests on beliefs about the lawlike behavior of physical objects; it is itself a particular instance of a law. And to support the weaker claim, 2U, one needs to couple the original two facts to a principle like:

(2L)   If, in circumstances like those that obtained, a force equal to the force I applied were applied to an object having the properties (e.g., weight) of the pissoir, then the object would not be budged.

To put the matter crudely, one has to suppose that it was not just an accident or random event that the pissoir did not

---

* N.B.: This case differs from one in which I claim (a): I tried my utmost (or, my best) to budge it, and (b): I failed to budge it. It might reasonably be held that a and b entail 2, but if so, then a is equivalent to (a1): I did everything I could to budge it. Here the modal proposition, 2, is being supported by another modal proposition, a (i.e., a1), so the real problems are only shifted from the conclusion, 2, to the premise, a1.

budge when I tried to budge it that time. If the behavior of objects under force were random, if, everything else being the same, sometimes an object moves and sometimes it doesn't, then it would not be true that I couldn't budge it then. And obviously part of our conception of the physical world (our common-sense Theory about physical objects) is that objects don't behave that way.

Ultimately and essentially what is at stake here is nothing less (and nothing more) than the naturalistic fallacy. At issue is whether and how a modal proposition is derivable from a set of factual propositions. The solution I am offering is that the connection is made—always and only—within a System. Or rather, what I am offering is not a solution but a realignment of a problem, which, depending on what one thought the problem was, either exposes it as a pseudo problem or transforms it into a genuine, challenging philosophical problem about the construction and constituents of an adequate System (e.g., a moral code).

Let us begin at the beginning with this infamous passage from Hume:

I cannot forbear adding to these reasonings an observation, which may, perhaps, be found of some importance. In every system of morality, which I have hitherto met with, I have always remark'd, that the author proceeds for some time in the ordinary way of reasoning, and establishes the being of a God, or makes observations concerning human affairs; when of a sudden I am surpriz'd to find, that instead of the usual copulations of propositions, *is*, and *is not*, I meet with no proposition that is not connected with an *ought*, or an *ought not*. This change is imperceptible; but it is, however, of the last consequence. For as this *ought*, or *ought not* expresses some new relation or affirmation, 'tis necessary that it shou'd be observ'd and explain'd; and at the same time that a reason should

The Modals and Morality

be given, for what seems altogether inconceivable, how this new relation can be a deduction from others, which are entirely different from it. But as authors do not commonly use this precaution, I shall presume to recommend it to the readers; and am persuaded, that this small attention wou'd subvert all the vulgar systems of morality, and let us see, that the disinction of vice and virtue is not founded merely on the relations of objects, nor is perceiv'd by reason.[6]

Though abundantly obscure in its details, this passage undeniably contains three claims. First, there is a problem about deducing propositions containing 'ought' from propositions containing not 'ought' but 'is'. I would agree; there is a problem. Second, an understanding of this problem reveals something about the nature of morality, and third, the problem is essentially a logico-semantic one turning on the meaning of 'ought'. To my knowledge every meta-ethicist has accepted the last two claims. And my contention is that those two claims are now incompatible. (I say "now" because once upon a time the meaning of 'ought' might have revealed something about the nature of a culture's moral code.)

I am going to construct a logico-semantic principle and call it the Principle of the Naturalistic Fallacy (hereafter, PNF). The title is apt because an inference of an 'ought' proposition from an 'is' proposition is invalid only if it violates this principle. Yet, some meta-ethicists might complain of the name because of some peculiarities of my PNF. First, it says nothing about 'ought' specifically; instead it is phrased in terms of modal propositions in general, since any philosophically interesting point about 'ought' applies to 'must' and 'can' as well. Secondly, my PNF says nothing about 'good' or 'right' or normative terms or value judgments. As such it deviates from the post-Humean conception of the naturalistic fallacy—but if that be a bar to its title, then philosophers are being rather friv-

The Significance of Sense

olous when claiming that the fallacy is a violation of a *logico-semantic* principle. From the linguistic standpoint, the class of words or utterances philosophers have had in mind is a rag-bag collection, and I see no semantic or syntactic principles applying to all and only members of that class.* (Thus, a separate argument has to be constructed for 'right' and 'wrong' in the next chapter.) Thirdly, my PNF neither says nor implies anything about morality or value—but if that deprives it of the title of a PNF then there is no naturalistic fallacy to commit, for no legitimate logico-semantic principle governing the modals has implications about morality or value.

My PNF is a simple, four-part unpacking of my modal definitions:

I.   'n v' entails 'n can v'.

II.   The joint truth of j-jjjj entails the correlative proposition 'n must v' (*Mutatis mutandis* for the other modals.)

III.   If j-jjjj are each true, then any one of them implies the correlative proposition 'n must v'. (*Mutatis mutandis* for the other modals.)

IV.   A predicate 'F' is such that 'Fn' entails 'n must v' only if j-jjjj must be true for 'F' to be truly predicated of n. (*Mutatis mutandis* for the other modals.)

The elaboration that follows serves to connect these parts to philosophical tradition; many details and niceties irrelevant

---

* For example, what do 'ought' and 'good' share which would be relevant to the naturalistic fallacy? Both are often alleged to be normative terms and to be commonly used in value judgments, but as regards 'ought' this seems patently false—though it is a moot point until these bits of meta-ethical jargon ('normative term', 'value judgment') are given usable definitions. No such problems plague the word 'evaluation' and its cognates, and it seems clear that, except in sentences like 'That steak ought to cost only three dollars.', 'ought' has little to do with evaluations, whereas 'good' has a good deal to do with them.

to the naturalistic fallacy are ignored. The focus of the discussion is on the ways in which a modal proposition is legitimately inferable from a nonmodal proposition. I call a proposition modal if it contains (used, not mentioned) the words 'must', 'can', or 'ought' or their negations or synonyms (e.g., 'have to', 'may', 'should') or their nonauxiliary verb counterparts (e.g., 'necessarily', 'possible').

I. The nonmodal proposition 'n v' entails the correlative modal proposition 'n can v' and all modal propositions entailed by it. This is of limited interest because the chain of entailments is restricted, and, since 'n v' must be connected to the same System as the entailed 'n can v', the fact that n is actually v does not itself show that n can v when the relevant System is an SI (any SI, not just a moral one).

II. Since j-jjjj constitutes the definition of 'n must v', the joint truth of the nonmodal propositions j-jjjj entails the truth of the correlative modal proposition 'n must v' and all modal propositions entailed by it. And since each of j-jjjj may be entailed by other nonmodal propositions and implied by still others, there is a large number of nonmodal propositions whose truth constitutes sufficient grounds for the truth of 'n must v'. The same can be said of the relations between l-lll and 'n can v', k-kkkk and 'n cannot v' and 'n must not v', and m-mmm and 'n ought to v'. To simplify matters, let us concentrate on the relation of j-jjjj to 'n must v'.

Anyone seriously concerned with the *genuine* issues of philosophy in general and ethics in particular could agree to II even where the relevant System is a moral code just because it leaves those issues untouched. The moral issues—I mean the personal and political ones we confront in our lives— normally lead to a scrutiny of the truth of the particular jj, jjj, and jjjj without discussing j (i.e., whether there is an adequate moral System). This is a consequence of two obvious (though not trivial) facts. First, having a moral argument presupposes having (believing) some moral System, just as having an argument about anything presupposes having the relevant kind of System. Second, the mass of moral discourse takes place among speakers sharing highly similar moral Systems, just as the mass of discourse about anything at all takes place among speakers sharing highly similar relevant Systems. Radical advances in transportation and communication have altered this somewhat, as has the spread of anti-authoritarian educational practices. Nevertheless, it is still largely true. As a result we rarely question whether the specific System we are using is adequate, let alone whether any System of that kind is adequate.

On the other hand, philosophical ethics has always centered on the truth of j, and to a lesser extent, jjj. The philosophical problems of ethics—epistemological, metaphysical, and moral —are, I suggest, best understood as problems about the existence, nature, construction, and contents of an adequate moral System. In effect, moral skepticism deals with whether there exists an adequate moral System, and (supposing that there does) whether and how we can know which Systems are adequate. Similarly, in the main, relativism and subjectivism are concerned with whether there are grounds for preferring one moral System over another, and, if there are, whether those grounds are sufficient to rule out all but one System as inadequate. On a different level, the debate between deontologists and consequentialists is most perspicuously pictured as an argument over the construction and contents of an adequate moral System. And on yet another level, the determination of the existence of such things as the Form of the Good and non-natural moral qualities is most manageably treated as a problem in Theory construction concerned with the entities required by an adequate moral System. I am saying that moral philosophy has, in effect, always concerned itself with the requirements and construction of an adequate moral System. I am also saying that it should, more explicitly, continue to do so.

Nothing distinctive about morality is at stake here. Philosophy, as a whole and in its specialties, has been and should be principally an investigation into the requirements and construction of adequate Systems of all kinds (though not every kind). To be sure, Anglo-American philosophers eschew on principle or simply ignore the tasks of *constructing* certain kinds of Systems. Of late, philosophers of history have grown timid in reaction to the excesses of their predecessors. Yet their colleagues in the philosophy of the physical sciences frequently explore the substantive claims of scientific Theories, and this practice is taken as a matter of course among philosophers of mathematics, psychology, religion, law, language, and aesthetics. The practices of philosophers of different disciplines seem more a function of the differing evolutions of the separate disciplines than of some difference in the logic of those disciplines.

To repeat, my point is that the PNF and the meanings of the modals have no bearing on the existence, requirements, nature, construction, or constituents of an adequate System of any kind, including a moral one. For this reason my account of the modals is, as any proper account of them must be, completely neutral as regards the genuine issues of philosophy. Even an extreme moral skeptic could accept my account since it leaves completely open (as it must) whether any moral System is adequate. Perhaps the very idea of such a System is ultimately incoherent; I doubt it, but it remains to be shown one way or the other—but not by an investigation into the meaning of the modals. As far as semantics goes, the existence and nature of an adequate moral System is the same kind of problem as the existence and nature of an adequate physical System.

My account should be unacceptable only to philosophers who have worried about which constraints are put on an adequate moral System by the meaning of 'ought' and the PNF. My position is threefold: first, any constraints put on by 'ought' would be put on by 'must' and 'can'; second, any constraints any of these words put on a moral System would be put on any System; third, none of these words put any constraints on any System. If this position is sound, what follows immediately is not so much that certain ethical theories are incorrect, as that they have been defended with bogus arguments. That is, philosophers have sought a definition of 'ought', not in a spirit of autotelicism (or so one hopes), but as a key to the nature of morality. So, what they have wanted to conclude may be correct even granting everything I have said. But this concession will little mollify many meta-ethicists since all their arguments for those conclusions are, in one way or another, based on an erroneous conception of the implications of the PNF.

Curiously, Hume is an exception. Though he is the founder of the fallacy, he relied on another set of arguments to show what his successors tried to show with a PNF. But his arguments are equally bad; they require a fundamentally incoherent conception of human psychology, one which divorces Reason from the Passions. And while Hume saw that, given this picture, Reason could not conflict with the Passions, he failed to see that, given this picture, Reason could no more accord with or help the Passions than it could conflict with or hinder them. It is totally inexplicable how Hume's impotent Reason is to affect the Passions at all, even to inform them of the best means for achieving some desired end. For those Passions are blind and deaf, so how are they to be instructed? Given Hume's picture, the relation between facts and desires, between facts and the "hypothetical 'ought' " is just as mysterious as the relation between facts and the desirable, between facts and the "categorical 'ought' ".

Still, Hume seems far wiser than his successors who have been struck by the fact of moral disagreement, and have thought a PNF somehow explained those disagreements and showed them to be unsettleable by rational means. They have thought that every 'ought' proposition is supportable only by another 'ought' proposition and that the last link in the chain hangs unsupported.[7] But if that explained moral disagreements, it would also explain disagreements over modal propositions connected to other Systems, and thus one would expect those disputes to be as common and continuous as they are in morals. But Hume was impressed, perhaps more than any philosopher before or since, with the phenomenon of widespread *agreement* on moral issues. He was right to be so impressed. Given the deep and abiding disparities and conflicts among men in tastes and desires, information and intelligence, situations and aspirations, it is truly remarkable that men do so often agree—and, more remarkable still, that where there is disagreement assent can sometimes be compelled by argument. Once the primitive Freudian and S-R learning theories are abandoned, the phenomenon of agreement becomes far more surprising than that of disagreement. Neither phenomenon is explicable by reference to the meaning of the modals. Of course, agreement on the truth of a proposition depends in part on agreement upon the meanings of the terms, but this is true of any proposition—and is as true of genuine disagreement as of genuine agreement. In general, the source of agreement and *apparently* unsettleable disagreement lies in the Systems espoused by the disputants. I say "apparently", because what appears to be evidence of unsettleability may be only evidence of the enormous difficulty of showing one System to be superior to another.

III: If j-jjjj are each true, then the truth of any of these nonmodal propositions implies the truth of 'n must v' and all modal propositions entailed by it. Note, when defending a modal proposition like 'n must v', normally we assert only jj (i.e., 'Fn'). Generally we don't assert anything like jjjj (i.e., 'C obtains') unless and until some reason is given to doubt it. Less frequently do we need to say anything like jjj, and j is rarely stated outside the context of a philosophical debate. I mention this because the usual versions of the PNF focus on the relation of the modal proposition to jj or to jj conjoined with propositions describing the rest of the state of affairs. (The latter would be roughly equivalent to 'C obtains'.) That is, when philosophers talk of factual propositions they usually have in mind propositions like jj and jjjj (or some set of propositions equivalent to them). And while such propositions do not entail a modal proposition, they do imply it, and do so without presupposing some modal proposition. More, any factual proposition implies some modal proposition in every kind of System. Suppose some proposition jj is true. Then, for any System, if j, jjj, and jjjj are also true then jj implies 'n must v'. If j is false then jj implies 'n can v', and if j is true and either jjj or jjjj is false then j implies '—(must v)'. Thus the question is not *whether* a factual proposition implies a modal proposition, but *which* ones it does imply. And so, once granted that an adequate moral System exists, the problem is not whether factual propositions can imply an 'ought' proposition of a moral System, but which 'ought' propositions are implied by which factual propositions. The solution—in a moral as in any other kind of System—is found by an investigation of the contents of an adequate System.

Let me trace a route to a muddle that meta-ethicists may have trod. In the normal course of speech we produce a number of factual propositions (jj and jjjj) and then infer a modal proposition or first produce a modal proposition and, when challenged, produce some factual propositions. (See the quotation from Hume.) If pressed further we cite certain laws of the relevant System (i.e., jjj). But frequently we do not formulate the laws as I have done; instead we use a modal sentence. So it looks as though the factual propositions provide grounds for a modal proposition only if some modal proposition is presupposed. So far this story could be told of any kind of System. What distinguishes a moral System is that in other Systems (especially SA's) it is also natural to state the laws as I have done, namely, without modal terms. Thus the modal propositions connected with other Systems do not seem so problematic. Further, as I have said, the natural way to formulate a moral law is with an 'ought', not a 'must' or 'can'. So it looks as though 'ought' has some special semantic relation to a moral System. Finally it is far from obvious how one is to show that some purported moral law is genuine, one that would belong to an adequate moral System. Given all this, it is understandable why one might think that the relation of factual judgments to the modal judgments of a moral System is a special puzzle, and that the puzzle has something to do with the meaning of 'ought'.

The Significance of Sense

I don't deny that the relation of factual judgments to moral judgments is problematic. But (contra intuitionsts and non-cognitivists) the problem is not semantical; more precisely, it has nothing to go with the meaning of 'ought' or the other modals. (The next chapter makes the parallel point about 'right' and 'wrong'.) And since the problem is not semantical, neither (contra some naturalists) is its solution: adducing a handful of predicates with interesting entailments, even if successful, leaves the general problem untouched (see pp. 172–174). But to show a problem to be badly formulated is not to solve or dissolve it: strategies such as exhibiting the univocity of modal terms or debunking the use of 'factual' ('descriptive') and 'value' ('normative') as designating mutually exclusive or jointly exhaustive categories of terms and judgments are only delaying tactics. There is a problem, both genuine and philosophical, about the justification of moral judgments, but in essentials neither the problem nor its solution is unique to an adequate moral System.

The problem does not concern the semantic interrelations of a System's lexicon; in its most general form it can be abstracted from the contents of a System altogether. The problem is statable and best understood without reference to any particular lexical items because it concerns the logic of justifying any judgment of a System. That is, it concerns the structural properties of Systems.

From my account it should be obvious that in any System the justification of a modal judgment hinges on the justification of the correlative 'n v' (or '—(n v)'), which in turn depends upon the justification of 'Fn ⊃ Vn' in the relevant System, and that in turn raises the issue of the justification of '(x)(Fx ⊃ Vx)'. (The complications involving the Circumstances C can safely be ignored here.) In any System, a law may be justified by derivation from other laws of the System, but since that process must end at some point we may as well suppose we are there already. So we are left with the problem of describing how a purported law is to be shown to be a genuine law of an adequate relevant System.

The appropriate justification procedure is a function of the structure of the System. Another classification of Systems comparable to that marked by the SA-SI distinction is needed here. I call a System a Conventional System (hereafter, CS) if the truth of a law of the System, '$(x) (Fx \supset Vx)$', is a condition of the truth of its instantiatable judgments, '$(Fa \supset Va) (Fb \supset Vb)$ . . .'. Thus, the truth of the judgments is a consequence of the truth of the laws, and the latter is a consequence of something else. Legal Systems, games, codes of etiquette, and languages are CS's. I call a System a Natural System (hereafter, NS) if it is not a CS. Here, though a law entails its instantiatable judgments and thus can be used to justify them, its truth is not a condition of their truth. Adequate physical, logical, and moral Systems are NS's.

This distinction will seem most obscure if the traditional philosophical conception of a condition is employed rather than the ordinary one I have described in my article "Conditions." According to the traditional conception, the condition relation is defined by material implication so that P is a sufficient condition of Q if and only if Q is a necessary condition of P, and thus P is a necessary and sufficient condition of Q if and only if Q is a necessary and sufficient condition of P. But according to me, all that is mistaken; if P is a condition of Q, then Q is a consequence of P. The condition relation is transitive, asymmetrical, and irreflexive. It involves a relation of dependency; if P is a sufficient condition of Q or if Q is a necessary condition of P, then '$p \supset q$' is true, but it must also be true that, e.g., Q obtains in virtue (or, as a result) of P obtaining or Q must obtain in order that P obtain.

Like the SA-SI distinction, the CS-NS distinction is meant to capture a venerable intuitive idea, hopefully with some degree of precision. So too, the CS-NS distinction is not semantical; an unambiguous sentence can express a law in both a CS (e.g., a language) and an NS (e.g., a linguistic Theory). Whether a specific System is a CS or an NS is a matter of how the laws are in fact used, but whether an adequate System of a certain kind is a CS or an NS is determined by the requirements of an adequate System of that kind. Many and perhaps all moral Systems actually held are, in one way or another and to one extent or another, CS's; moralities in which the laws are a consequence of custom or divine command are only the most obvious examples. But all such moralities are inadequate because an adequate moral System is an NS.

In a CS the truth of a law is a condition of the truth of its instantiatable judgments:* e.g., it is true that I must curb my dog (i.e., if I am walking a dog, then (ideally) I curb the dog) in virtue of the fact that there is an ordinance that dogs must be curbed (i.e., it is true that dogs must be curbed). The converse is not true: the fact that I must curb my dog may be used as *evidence* that there is a law, but the existence of the law is a consequence, not of that fact, but of an act of legislation by the city council.†

---

* A reminder: Although *qua* statute, judicial ruling, etc., an utterance lacks a truth-value, a truth-value is assignable to what is said (Cf. pp. 70–75, 119–121, 136), and is so even if an imperative sentence is used (See pp. 139–140).

† Even when a consequence of a judge's ruling in a particular case is, in effect, the establishment of a law, the logic (if not the psychologic) of the situation is the same, for the judge finds that the particular act before him is, e.g., illegal because it is an act of a certain character, and

The Modals and Morality

In a CS, to say that a law (i.e., a statement of the law) is true is to say that there is such a law of the System. The truth and existence of the law is a consequence of the actions of the lawmaker, so to justify the truth of the law, to show that it is genuine, one must show that the lawmaker has, explicitly or implicity, made the law. This is done by, for example, consulting statute books. (Sometimes the process is quite complex and its outcome disputable, but the structure is unchanged.) To justify the truth of a law is not to justify the law, it is not to show that the law ought to exist (e.g., that it is not unjust). A legal System may require that the laws meet certain moral standards, but the moral considerations are legally relevant if and only if the lawmaker makes them be so. If the lawmaker does not make them be so then the System may be inadequate, but even in an adequate CS the moral considerations are relevant if and only if the lawmaker makes them be so.

The lawmaker of a CS may be an individual, organization, or community. In the main the laws are made by an act of legislation as in formal legal Systems and games or by customary acceptance and practice as in natural languages and codes of etiquette. In any CS the law *qua* law is akin to a generalized command, but this may be a misleading way of talking, especially about linguistic rules and the like which exist in virtue of their observance. Still, such laws belong to a CS, and thus to an SI. The law, '(ideally) (x) $(Fx \supset Vx)$', is still a condition,

---

not that acts of this character are illegal because this one is. The judge's decision has two consequences: that acts of a certain character are illegal, and, as a consequence of that, that this act is illegal. What law (if any) has thereby been created may be disputable; the relevant characteristics of the action may be in doubt. Subsequent jurists may disagree as to the evidential relation of the original ruling to a law and to the illegality of similar but slightly different acts. However, such disputes do not question whether a law is *presupposed* by the original decision.

not a consequence of the truth of its instantiatable judgments, '((ideally) Fa ⊃ Va)((ideally) Fb ⊃ Vb) . . .', even though it is a consequence of the truth of '((in fact) Fa ⊃ Va)((in fact) Fb ⊃ Vb) . . .'. Of course, the law is also a consequence of the fact that if '(in fact) Fd. —Vd' is true then —Vd is criticized. Thus, to say 'We don't do (say) . . .' can be to criticize via stating a regularity. Note that a social scientific System (e.g., a linguistic Theory), an SA that is an NS, may have laws which mirror the laws of such CS's. But there the truth of a law, 'in fact) (x) (Fx ⊃ Vx)', is a consequence, not a condition, of the truth of its instantiatable judgments, '((in fact) Fa ⊃ Va) ((in fact) Fb ⊃ Vb) . . .'.

The traditional conception of the CS-NS distinction has, quite understandably, become associated with various other oppositions. Such associations must be resisted. For instance, universal or necessary acceptance of a law is not a sign of an NS. Even if some laws of natural languages are biologically determined by the human brain and thus common to all languages, languages are still CS's. So too, not being man-made or arbitrary is not a sign of an NS. The commands of a god might form a moral System, but the System is a CS because the truth of the laws is a consequence of the commands and a condition of the truth of their instantiatable judgments. Even if the laws are the terms of a Social Contract or are commanded by our own Reason (don't ask me how), the System is a CS for the structure is the same. Such Systems may share much of the content of an adequate moral System, an NS, but their structure is defective.

All SA's are NS's (NSA's) in which the truth of the instantiatable judgments is a condition, not a consequence of the truth of the laws. This derives from the nature of an SA: the truth of a law is assessed by reference to its instances and counterinstances. Because of the entailment relation, instantiatable judgments are justifiable by reference to the laws; we can make accurate and justified predictions and retrodictions on the basis of genuine laws of an NSA. (This is largely if not entirely the point of discovering such laws in the first place.) Still, ultimately the truth-value of a law is judged by the truth-value of its instantiatable judgments, not vice versa.

Assessing a purported law of an NSA involves two broad kinds of problems. First, the general problems of Theory construction: the problems of assessing a purported law given the truth of some of its instantiatable judgments. As Hume noticed, the truth of a partial list of instantiatable judgments provides only a necessary not a sufficient condition of the truth of the generalization. Thus, no set of data (examined instances of a law) constitutes logically sufficient evidence for a law having unexamined instances. Further, as Goodman showed, since an unlimited number of predicates are truly predicable of such data, the data provides a necessary condition of the truth of a variety of incompatible laws, but not a sufficient condition of any. Moreover, even if all the instantiatable judgments are known to be true, the generalization may fail to be a genuine law; other considerations may be relevant to the assessment of the law (See pp. 39–41). These problems of Theory construction are describable without reference to the content of any NSA or even to the unique structure of an NSA; not surprisingly then, such problems recur in various forms in any NS and many CS's.* The so-

---

* E.g., Wittgenstein, developing the same insight as Goodman, showed that, although the acceptance of a rule (e.g., a law of a language) is a logically necessary and sufficient condition of the correctness of its applications (the instantiatable judgments), what rule is accepted is never uniquely specifiable because any signs used to state or explain the rule are variously interpretable and any finite set of actual applications is a necessary condition of the existence of an unlimited number of rules but not a sufficient condition of the existence any. Thus, any new application

lution of such problems is the task of SI's such as inductive logic.

The other batch of problems concern the determination of the truth-value of the instantiatable judgments. In any NSA the truth of 'Fa ⊃ Va' is a consequence of the fact that if (in fact) Fa, then (in fact) Va, and that fact is established ultimately by some set of observations. However, the paths by which the truth of a judgment is linked to certain observations will vary with the kind of NSA (e.g., psychology, history, physics), its content, and the particular predicates used in the judgment. The linkage may be of considerable complexity and may presuppose the truth of all sorts of laws, some of which may belong to that or other NSA's while others would be principles of logic and rules of evidence, laws of SI's.

What remains to be discussed are NS's that are SI's (NSI's). Such systems could, with some propriety, be called Systems of rationality, and their laws, principles of rationality. Included here are adequate moral, aesthetic, mathematical, deductive, and inductive logical Systems.

Before proceeding further, something should be said for my claim that logic and mathematics are SI's. My position here is essentially that of Wittgenstein in *Remarks on the Foundations of Mathematics*. In reaction to intuitionism and formalism he argues that the laws of mathematics and logic do not serve to describe the behavior of signs or the overt or mental be-

---

could be an ideal application (i.e., is a consequence of some rule that is a consequence of the actual applications); whether it is depends on whether it is accepted as such. (Incidentally, this may create problems for Goodman's solution to his own problem: whatever difficulties attach to projecting that emeralds are green instead of grue attach to projecting that our predicate 'green' is not some grue-like predicate. What is entrenched is the sign; the meaning of 'green', what we will count as members of its extension is as much in doubt as the color of emeralds.)

havior of human or mechanical computors. Nor do they describe the properties or behavior of physical objects (à la Mill) or transphysical entities (à la Plato). We treat the laws as norms.

We can, of course, say that, e.g., arithmetic laws describe the properties of numbers and that numbers exist. That is, we can treat the laws not as norms but as descriptions of the properties of objects in an ideal realm of numbers just as, for example, moral laws can be treated as descriptions of the properties (behavior) of objects with a holy will in an ideal realm, a Kingdom of Ends. So conceived, an SI is an SA, and to say here that *in fact* such and such is to say that such and such obtains in the relevant ideal realm. This conception is altogether natural and can be harmless when restricted to activities such as pure mathematics.* The resistance to this picture is not a bias for spatio-temporal physical reality as a paradigm of existence. What is problematic is the application of this picture to our actual use of mathematics and other NSI's. Even after putting aside the permanent enigma of how we could ever know what transpires in such supra-sensible realms, we are left with the problem of relating these truths to the physical world, but any procedure for relating them would presuppose their applicability to this world. The supposition of a realm in which NSI's are NSA's is idle.†

---

* However, to say, e.g., 'There exists a prime number between 4 and 6.' would normally be taken as a statement *within* a mathematical System, as a law of the System. It need not suggest anything about the nature of the System. By contrast, a statement such as 'Numbers are entities without spatio-temporal location.' is not a mathematical law.

† I offer the following as evidence that logic and mathematics are SI's. Whenever 'can' is used in the context of either System it is interchangeable with 'may', but 'can' is interchangeable with 'may' only in the context of an SI. Turning it around, when used in the context of mathe-

The Significance of Sense

We treat the laws of logic and mathematics as norms. They can be violated by computors (mechanical or mammalian), and when they are we correct the computation and the computor, not the law. There cannot be actual counterinstances to the laws because they are norms governing our conception, and hence our perception and description of any kind of thing. Thus, if we apply them faithfully, we do not count anything as being a counterinstance. True, we may also reject descriptions of events which would falsify a well-accepted SA law, but here we are led not by the SA law itself, but by some SI law, e.g., some rule of Theory construction such as Quine's "maxim of minimal mutilation." True too, these norms may not be eternally unrevisable; experience might lead us to alter them—but not by falsifying them. The laws of an NSI differ from those of an NSA not merely in degree of alterability but also in kind. The difference is that given in the definitions of an SI and an SA.

Now, what is the truth of an NSI law a consequence of? In the case of logical and mathematical laws the perennial answers are the world or language. But to suppose that they are true in virtue of the facts of this or some other world is to suppose that these Systems are SA's, and to suppose that they are true in virtue of the acceptance of linguistic rules is to suppose that they are CS's. And to suppose that since such laws are logically implied by any statement they are true in virtue of anything and everything is to suppose that the condition relation is simply a truth-functional relation. So too for any NSI: e.g., if moral laws were true in virtue of some special kind of facts, a moral System would be an SA, and if they were true in virtue of being commanded, accepted, or the like by gods or men then a moral System would be a CS.

---

matics or logic 'may' never has its likelihood indicator except when one is predicting the yet unknown outcome of performing a certain operation: e.g., 'This conclusion might be derivable from those five premises.'.

168

The Modals and Morality

What are the conditions of the truth of an NSI law? The proper answer is: Nothing. Uniting the properties of an NS and an SI precludes there being something in virtue of which the laws of the System are true.* The arguments showing that an adequate System of a certain kind is an NSI may differ for different kinds of Systems (I have not produced such arguments), but, given that a System is an NSI, the truth of its laws is not a consequence of anything. Put it this way. We suppose that, in some intuitive sense, the laws of NSI's are necessary truths. That need imply nothing about how or whether we know such truths. It may imply only that they are not contingent (i.e., contingent upon something else) truths, that they are not *dependent* upon anything—which is to say that nothing is a condition of their being true. (We could define a necessary truth as one that has no conditions.) Put it another way: NSI's form the framework of all our knowledge, but they do not and cannot have a foundation.

How is an NSI law justified? Not by showing that the conditions of its truth obtain, but that is not the only form of justification. We can, for example, derive the law from other laws, but here we are supposing that that process has come to an end. What more can be done? What more *is* done?

Goodman has contended that we justify a deduction (an instantiatable judgment) by showing it to be an instantiation of a law of a System of deductive logic, and we justify a rule (law) by showing that its instantiatable judgments (deductive inferences) are ones "we actually make and sanction."

If a rule yields inacceptable inferences, we drop it as invalid. Justification of general rules thus derives from judgments rejecting or accepting particular deductive inferences. . . . (R)ules and particu-

---

* A trivial exception: The truth of any statement is a consequence of what is stated being the case (e.g., 'Snow is white.' is true is virtue of snow being white).

lar inferences alike are justified by being brought into agreement with each other. *A rule is amended if it yields an inference we are unwilling to accept; an inference is rejected if it violates a rule we are unwilling to amend.* The process of justification is the delicate one of making mutual adjustments between rules and accepted inferences; and in the agreement achieved lies the only justification needed for either.[8]

Goodman restates this same justification procedure for the laws of inductive logic and their instantiatable judgments.

The claim of completeness aside, Goodman's description seems accurate. The Systems' status as NS's is sustained, for it is not suggested that the laws or their instantiatable judgments are true in virtue of being accepted or that one is true in virtue of the other. But so described, the procedure seems suspiciously devoid of rationality at its center: nothing is said regarding any rational constraints on or reasons for our initial acceptance of certain judgments and laws, nor for our unwillingness to accept certain judgments or amend certain laws when conflicts become manifest. It appears that we could be guaranteed of, at most, only internal consistency.

Rawls [9] fills in some of the pieces while presenting a justification procedure for a moral System. (He too claims a parallel with the procedure for inductive logic.) He defines a class of considered judgments of competent (moral) judges. The defining criteria are common-sense principles we would and do use to determine a subclass of judgments which are most likely to be correct (e.g., the judge is of at least normal intelligence; the judgment is made after careful reflection) plus some heuristic restrictions (e.g., the judgments are not based on a systematic and conscious use of laws of the System). Roughly, the criteria are ones whose nonsatisfaction we use to explain or excuse a failure of reasoning or judgment. Special criteria may be needed for some Systems but not others (e.g., a certain degree of sensitivity for moral judgments). Given all this, an adequate (moral) System is a simple, comprehensive, and manageable set of laws which have among their instantiatable judgments the considered judgments of competent (moral) judges. Then, unless the initial class of judgments is rendered consistent without recourse to laws conflicting with subsequent judgments, the process of adjustment Goodman describes must be engaged in until we achieve a state Rawls calls reflective equilibrium. A law of an adequate NSI as determined by this procedure is a genuine law of the System. The appropriateness of this procedure for NSI's is part of what is suggested by calling their laws principles of rationality.

All too obviously, legitimate questions remain; the procedure is far from complete. I pick out three subsidiary issues for consideration now. First, the justification procedure might seem to enshrine moral conservatism. It does so only to the extent that any critique of a morality does; even the most radical reformers appeal, of necessity, to already well-accepted premises (i.e., moral laws or judgments).

Second, some philosophers balk at talk of moral laws (rules, principles, etc.), especially at the seemingly indiscriminate talk in which I have indulged. I sympathize entirely with their complaint but regard it as an ill-expressed insight. My specification of an NSI and its justification procedure makes no *suggestio falsi* regarding our cognition or employment of any generalizations. Roughly, to impute to someone a belief in certain moral laws, to say that they are in his moral System is only to abstract some patterns within his moral judgments taken as a whole; I merely assume that he accepts the logical and moral principle of treating similar cases in similar ways. The complaint has considerable force against those who, in effect, model moral laws on the laws of a legal System or other CS; a moral judgment is not true in virtue of a moral law it instantiates and need not be made with any reference to any particular generalization. Nevertheless, justification by instantiation from an accepted generalization is a form of justification.

Finally, although moral, logical, and mathematical Systems are NSI's, the former is commonly thought arbitrary (relative, subjective, etc.) whereas the latter pair are not. Perhaps the following will avail as an explanation. Mathematical and logical laws are disobeyed in word only; they have no genuine counter-instances. Without being descriptions of regularities, they form a framework for such descriptions and thus *seem* consistently verified by experience. But moral laws can be and, it pains me to relate, often are violated.* And thus, given our predilection for foundations of our beliefs, we most naturally incline to think of logic and mathematics as SA's and of morality as a CS; the latter, but not the former, is understandably associated with the arbitrary, the relative, and the like. Moreover, since the moralities we actually live by are largely CS's, the impression of something nonrational is close to irresistible.†

IV: I said in III that a factual proposition, jj, can only imply, not entail, a modal proposition. However, some factual proposi-

---

* Cf. Wittgenstein: "When an ethical law of the form 'Thou shalt . . .' is laid down, one's first thought is, 'And what if I do not do it?' " [10]

† So too with philosophical theories about the nature of morality; usually they maintain their grasp that morality is an SI, but, feeling unsteady without a foundation, they invent one (e.g., a command, a pro-attitude), thereby construing morality as a CS. But philosophers are a wily and bold lot and not easily deceived by appearance; many would sooner invent new kinds of facts or even whole new worlds and suitable powers of cognition—thereby rendering morality an SA—than forsake

tions like 'It is portable.' *seem* to entail some modal propositions like 'It can be carried (easily).'. This points to an over simplification, or—if you prefer—a fiction residing in my account, for I have talked as though there is always and everywhere a sharp distinction between what I call a Fact and what I call a System. The Facts are the particular facts about the object n and the System provides the structure in which these Facts have certain implications. Yet, since Facts are often, and perhaps always, Theory-laden, the distinction becomes somewhat tenuous. For one thing, it is sometimes a difficult or even futile task to distinguish between a Fact and a law of a System. (At this point the issues surrounding the analysis of dispositional terms relate to my account.) For another thing, what gets called a Fact may presuppose a particular Theory (which may or may not be adequate) that provides a particular vocabulary and a structuring of the world. Just because we hold to a certain Theory we are led to perceive the world in certain ways, and to accept certain descriptions. Consequently a revision or replacement of a Theory is accompanied by a shift in what we accept as Facts, and in the vocabulary we use to describe them.[11] (N.B.: Such considerations lend weight to my insistence on interpreting not only the modal propositions, but also the correlative 'n v' propositions in terms of the relevant Systems.)

Some of this is illustrated by an examination of Kirilov's remark, 'Everything is permitted.'. Kirilov believes that the truth of that remark is a consequence of the nonexistence of God, of nothing being forbidden. But permission requires a hierarchical System just as much as prohibition does. Thus, by his utterance he reveals what his whole life illustrates; he is still

---

an NS morality. The eclectic Kant may have managed both mistakes: a CSI morality for this realm, an NSA morality for another.

unable to accept his emancipation since he has yet to free himself from precisely what kept him captive—his own conception of his universe. If Kirilov were, in every sense of the word, a *free* thinker he would conclude that everything can be done, not that he is permitted to do everything. Instead, as his remark makes evident, he still conceives of himself in *terms* of being subject to an externally imposed System of legislation. The death of the Legislator has not abolished the System; instead, the anarchist becomes his own despot—Kirilov must become God. He remains his own captive, but then it would be no mean feat for him to truly free himself. As Nietzsche saw, it is one thing to kill God; it is quite another to become a man. To do that one must overcome himself. It is not enough to reject an old System, for one will only be ensnared by it again. One must also construct and adopt a new System with a new vocabulary, and a new vision of the universe and oneself.

Though the issues here are many and complex, their bearing on the naturalistic fallacy is not. A proposition presupposing anything less than 'n must v' presupposes can at best imply (i.e., conjoined with the missing presupposition, entail) 'n must v'. A predicate 'F' is such that 'Fn' entails 'n must v' only if j-jjjj must be true for 'F' to be truly predicated of n. And, unless the relevant System is the language, the truth of 'Fn' cannot be established solely by appeal to ongoing linguistic usage (e.g., 'This is what we call 'F'.'), for the fact that a word is used a certain way does not show that the System in which it operates is adequate (i.e., that j is true). Whatever problems attend the proof of a modal proposition attend the proof of any proposition entailing it. In short, lexicography cannot do duty for Theory construction. Semantic relations are of relatively little importance in the construction and defense of a scientific Theory; they have no greater value for a moral System.

The Modals and Morality

But now, since I concede that Facts, Systems, and semantics are so interrelated that the boundaries between them may be so blurred in some areas as to be nonexistent, the question arises: What is the justification for insisting on a sharp distinction between the semantics of the modals and the features of the Systems within which they are used? This is not to ask if my account "fits the facts" of linguistic usage, for the question presupposes that that matter is taken care of. Rather, it requests a justification for describing the facts as I do. The problem is one of Theory construction; the relevant Theory is linguistics.

Linguistics is a behavioral science, and thus an adequate linguistic Theory requires the context of a more comprehensive Theory of human behavior, a general social science. And I submit that a linguistic Theory which distinguished between Systems and the semantics of the modals as I do would be more suitable for a general social science than one that did not. Here I must return to the developmental theories.

I described Piaget's achievement as a discovery of a progressive alteration of the child's *Systems*. Yet, one might interpret the phenomena Piaget observed as evidencing a progressive alteration of the child's language. That is, above and beyond the accumulation of vocabulary and the closer observance of grammatical rules, the child's semantic system undergoes a stage-by-stage evolution. Indeed, on Quinean principles of translation this seems the conclusion to draw, for Quine supposes that:

Assertions startlingly false on the face of them are likely to turn on hidden differences of language. This maxim is strong enough in all of us to swerve us even from the homophonic method that is so fundamental to the very acquisition and use of one's mother tongue.

The common sense behind this maxim is that one's interlocutor's silliness, beyond a certain point, is less likely than bad translation—or, in the domestic case, linguistic divergence.[12]

But if "silliness" is wanted, one need search no further than the mouth of the nearest child. Upon asking a young child to complete a sentence like 'Half 9 is not 4 because . . . ', one is likely to receive the response "because he can't count." [13]

So let us hypothesize that the structures of human conceptual Systems are fairly stable, but a systematic shift of our semantics causes our infantile beliefs to appear radically different from our adult beliefs. And, for the sake of argument, let us not ask if this hypothesis if falsifiable, but only suppose it to be unfalsified by the observed behavior of children. What then is wrong with this hypothesis? Agreed, no sober scientist would entertain it, but why not? Lexicographers would resent having to compile three or six dictionaries (depending on which theorist's stage divisions are correct) for *every* language, one for each stage—but perhaps it can't be avoided. And since my disagreement with Eichmann on civil disobedience turns on a stage, and therefore a linguistic difference, our disagreement would be only apparent—but science has surprised us before. We can ignore these matters and concentrate on the central defect of the hypothesis.

Its main fault is that, apart from being unfalsified, there is absolutely nothing to recommend it, for nothing can be done with it. Even supposing we were willing to say that the postulation of a semantic shift *explains* the phenomenon, we would be unable to do anything with such an explanation. It stands alone, unconnected to everything we know or claim to know about human life. We would, for example, want an explanation of this semantic shift, why it happens and why it invariably takes the form it does. But nothing suggests itself. On the other hand, Piaget's hypothesis is buttressed (or at least buttressable or falsifiable) on all sides by the best available biological, anthropological, and psychological theories. Moreover, he has a coherent and highly plausible explanation of why our mental evolution takes the form it does. In short, Piaget's hypothesis accommodates itself to a comprehensive social science; the alternative linguistic hypothesis does not.

The next step is crucial, but I have no support for it. All I can say is that, to the best of my knowledge, as soon as a child appears to understand the words 'must', 'can', and 'ought' (and this is fairly early) he uses them in connection with his Systems just as we do with ours. So my argument is that since the child is progressively altering his Systems and since he continues to use the modals in the same way in connection with each of his Systems, it is best to distinguish the semantics of the modals from the content and structure of the various Systems. And at the same time this constitutes the best possible reason for treating the modals as univocal: the kinds of Systems are different, the Systems of each kind radically change, but (as far as I have been able to determine) my definitions plot a persistent feature of their use.

Another reason for rejecting the semantic shift hypothesis is that the observed alterations have none of the earmarks of a definitional transformation. That is, we have a conception of what happens when a person misunderstands or misuses a word, how its occurrence is determined, what the speaker says and does upon discovering it, and so on. But the behavioral changes Piaget reports do not, in general, fit the patterns of semantic change. I say "in general" because Piaget himself argues that some semantic alterations are tied to the modifications of the Systems. For example, he claims that at the earliest stage the child uses the word 'lie' to mean any parentally forbidden utterance, and hence both lies and obscenities are called lies. At the second stage, 'lie' is predicated of any untruth, so that, while obscenities are not lies, both lies and mistakes are called lies. Not until the final stage does the child use the word as an adult does.[14]

But in this case Piaget's description deserves critical scrutiny. He takes it to be a *belief* of the child based on the acceptance of parental authority that it is wrong to lie, and he supposes that children accept but distort the *definition* of 'lie' in a way that accommodates that moral belief to their total belief structure. But why not say that, at least in the early stages, 'It is wrong to lie.' is an analytic statement for the child; he accepts it and is unable to imagine its being false? Perhaps the child's error is that of *believing* that obscenities or mistakes are wrong in just the same way and for the same reasons as lies are. Or why not deny that any definitional shift is ever involved? Perhaps no statement is accepted by the child solely in virtue of the meanings that the constituent terms have in his vocabulary. Instead, the child has a complex system or beliefs, one of which is maintained throughout his maturation while others are progressively modified. While I have no need to take sides on the word 'lie', I want to reject all of these positions when applied to the modals.

I want to say that the conjunction j-jjjj is a *definition* of the sentence-frame 'n must v'. However, paradoxical though it be, ultimately I am reluctant to say that they have the same meaning or are synonymous. After all, a sentence of the form 'n must v' is not likely to be paired to the correlative conjunctive sentence j-jjjj by the synonymy intuitions of native speakers, yet, I take it, when people talk about synonymy they have some such pairing in mind. Similarly, to call them synonymous suggests that 'n must v if and only if j-jjjj' is an analytic statement, and again the picture seems to be that a competent native speaker would immediately assent to that statement upon a careful inspection of the meanings of the constituent terms, but any such picture is unfaithful to the facts. On the other hand, I don't want to say that that statement expresses a *belief* of mine and others—no matter what the depth of the seating of the belief. I resist this Quinesque suggestion, not because it threatens my use of the notion of entailment (that impoverishment would at most be an inconvenience), but because my intuition is that to describe it as simply a belief is to misdescribe it. Ultimately I would say that the definiens states the logically necessary and sufficient conditions of the truth of the definiendum. The truth of 'n must v' is a consequence of the truth of j-jjjj. Thus, though the two sentences are necessarily extensionally equivalent, they cannot be synonymous. (See my article "Conditions.") However, since the definiens not only states the truth conditions, but also unpacks the intuitive idea of the definiendum and has numerous other important virtues as well, I think it fully proper to call this a definition.

My definitions are purely formal. They are designed to satisfy certain requirements while ignoring others, principally that the definitions conform to our immediate intuitions of synonymy. Hence they do not look like the normal definition or explanation of meaning one finds in a dictionary or gives to a child or a foreigner. They are not like what one would say if asked what 'must' or 'can' or 'ought' means. These and similar considerations disincline me to speak of synonymy and thus perhaps even of meaning in connection with these definitions. Nonetheless, if for some reason a philosopher wants a definition, I think this is the sort that will have the highest utility for him. For that matter, given my recent argument, I think they are the most perspicuous sort of definitions of these words for a linguistic theory as well. Let me make a more modest claim: they are adequate definitions and, to my knowledge, the best available.

The Significance of Sense

But, to reiterate my opening sentences, it is the moral, not the story that is of interest. I would be content if I have succeeded in showing that the energies of a serious moral philosopher would be misspent in attempting to improve on my account, whatever its flaws may be. It's not that I rest confident in the perfection of my account. No, I am confident that it is fraught with imperfections—but not, I think, any that materially affect the philosophical issues. My purposes in presenting my account are purely polemical; its flaws are fatal only if my readers still attach philosophical importance to determining whether it is flawed.

Five

'Right' and 'Wrong'

Wir den Gebrauch unserer Wörter nicht *übersehen.*—
Unserer Grammatik fehlt es an Übersichtlichkeit.
      —L. Wittgenstein, *Philosophical Investigations*

I SHALL present an account of 'right' and 'wrong' later in this chapter, but first I shall proceed with the main business at hand, which is to exhibit the philosophical sterility of such an account. For this purpose it will suffice, I take it, to convince my readers that, as regards the semantics of 'right' and 'wrong', whatever problems beset a proof that such-and-such is the morally 'right' thing to do also beset a proof that such-and-such is the right answer to some question or the right time now or the right thus-and-such for any thus-and-such you please.

'Right' and 'wrong' are syntactically equivalent and semantically antonymous. What I say about one applies, *mutatis mutandis,* to the other unless I specifically state otherwise.

I have said that 'right' and 'wrong' are univocal over those adjectival uses in which they are antonyms.* An innocuous

---

* I think they are univocal over their adjectival and adverbial uses combined, but I won't debate this stronger thesis since it introduces syntactical issues without contributing to the philosophical ones.

falsehood. Both words have a primary and a derivative sense whose relation parallels that of the senses of 'courageous', which is predicated of acts and of agents in virtue of their (disposition to perform certain) acts. In their derivative sense, 'right' and 'wrong' are predicated of an agent (including such agents as clocks that "tell" time) on the basis of the agent's saying or doing or agreeing with some further thing that is right or wrong in the primary sense of those words. Compare:

(100)   That clock is giving the wrong time.

(101)   That clock is wrong.

(102)   You did the right thing in agreeing to his proposal.

(103)   You were right to agree to his proposal.

(104)   You gave the right answer to question 5.

(105)   You were right about question 5.

The even numbered sentences use the primary sense; the odd use the derivative sense. If the subject is an agent, the derivative sense is used whenever 'right' or 'wrong' immediately precedes 'to VP', 'in *Gerund P*', 'about *NP*' or 'with *NP*'. The derivative sense cannot be used when a noun phrase immediately succeeds 'right' or 'wrong'. Finally, note that, unless the primary sense is really more than one sense, there is no reason to think that the derivative sense is really more than one sense. Henceforth I will attend to only the uses of the primary sense.

Take the class of cases in which 'right' or 'wrong' is immediately succeeded by a noun phrase. Upon inspection it appears that in all such cases the environment either is, or is an ellipsis of, or is easily transformed into the form:

(106)   NP$_1$ *copula* the right (wrong) NP$_2$ + *qualifying component.*

Various adjectival or adverbial phrases may appear either immediately succeeding or immediately preceding the 'the': e.g.,

'Right' and 'Wrong'

'not', 'quite', 'one of', 'morally', 'just', 'absolutely', 'precisely'. Except for one set of cases (see below), the qualifying component is always a 'for NP to VP' component. Here are some examples of some transformations. (Sometimes alternative transformations are given because I am unsure of the most satisfactory transformation and sometimes because the sentence is elliptical and has various possible completions.)

(107)   Although he wants to do the right thing, he is unable.

(107a) Although he wants to do that which is the right thing for him (or, one) to do, he is unable.

(107b) Although he wants to do the thing which is the right thing for him (or, one) to do, he is unable.

(108)   Is this the right place?

(108a) Is it the case that this is the right place for us to be at?

(109)   Avocado is the right color for this room.

(109a) Avocado is the right color for this room to have.

(109b) Avocado is the right color for this room to be painted.

(110)   Avocado is the right color to paint this room.

(110a) Avocado is the right color for you (or, one) to paint this room.

(110b) Avocado is the right color for this room to be painted.

(111)   Wrong moves never pay.

(111a) Moves which are the wrong moves for one to make never pay.

Apparently, in a select class of cases, instead of a 'for-to' component, an adverbial or prepositional phrase immediately succeeds the second noun phrase. Compare:

(112)   Seven o'clock is the right time for us to leave for the airport.

(113)   Seven o'clock is the right time now (or, at this moment).

(114)   Your name, rank, and serial number is the right answer for a soldier to give to the questions of his captors.

(115)   'Samuel Gompers' is the right answer to question 37.

I say that 113 and 115 are not completable by a 'for-to' component because I have found none that seems satisfactory. However, these alternative qualifying components can be used only if the second noun phrase is 'time', 'answer', 'explanation', 'solution', or 'result' (and perhaps a few others I have overlooked), and when these qualifying components are used with those nouns they serve the same function as the 'for-to' component, that of a definite description.

In some sentence-environments the 'for-to' component is a source of sentence ambiguity. In the sentence:

(116)   He brought the book for me to read.

the 'for-to' component may serve to answer either a 'why' question or a 'which' question. Compare:

(117)   Why did he bring the book? He brought it for me to read.

(118)   Which book did he bring? He brought the one for me to read.

But in sentences of form 106, the 'for-to' component can serve only to tell *which*; it cannot serve to tell *why*. Clearly the prepositional and adverbial phrases like 'to question 37' play the same role. Thus, in all form 106 sentences the qualifying component serves to specify or identify a member of the class designated by the second noun phrase. That is, the expression 'the NP$_2$ + *qualifying component*' acts as a definite description, and thus in sentences of the form:

'Right' and 'Wrong'

$$
(106a) \quad NP_1 \; copula \; the \; NP_2 + \begin{cases} (for \; NP_3 \; to \; VP \\ (PP \\ (Adv \; P \end{cases}
$$

what is being said is that the object referred to by NP_1 is identical with the object referred to by the second noun phrase *cum* qualifying component. And now note that the deletion of 'right' from a form 106 sentence produces a form 106a sentence with the same associable truth-conditions as the form 106 sentence.

(113) Seven o'clock is the right time now.
(113a) Seven o'clock is the time now.
(115) 'Samuel Gompers' is the right answer to question 37.
(115a) 'Samuel Gompers' is the answer to question 37.
(119) Queen's pawn is not the right opening for you to use.
(119a) Queen's pawn is not the opening for you to use.
(120) That is the morally right thing for you to do.
(120a) That is the moral thing for you to do.
(121) Morally that is the right thing for you to do.
(121a) Morally that is the thing for you to do.

Though I think 'wrong' is not synonymous with 'not right', I think it is permissible to delete 'wrong' from form 106 sentences by replacing it with 'not right' and then deleting 'right'. This is comparable to the move from 'p ≡ 'p' is true' to '−p ≡ 'p' is false', which seems legitimate even though 'false' is not synonymous with 'not true'.

I call this the E (eliminability)-feature of 'right' and 'wrong'. Further evidence both of the existence of the E-feature and of 'the NP_2 + *qualifying component*' being a definite description is obtained by an examination of the numerous alternative ways of saying what is said with a form 106 sentence:

(122)   That's (not) it.
(123)   That's (not) the one.
(124)   Thattaway. (That is the way.)

Though sentences 122–124 are not synonymous with any form 106 sentence (which would they be synonymous with?), they can be and often are used as substitutes for such sentences.

Such facts tell us a good deal about the use of 'right' when immediately preceding a noun phrase. For one thing it explains why the preceding article is normally 'the' and rarely 'a' and, if it is 'a', it can be transformed into 'one of the'. It now seems that this is not a property of 'right' per se, but is actually a feature of the definite descriptions in the context of which 'right' appears. Along with this it becomes clearer why 'right' is rarely used in its comparative and superlative forms.

More important for my purposes, such facts make it implausible to suppose that 'right' is ambiguous. I know of only one other word in English possessing the E-feature, the near synonym and etymologically related word, 'correct'. (Thus, it is both difficult and important to distinguish 'correct' from 'right'.) Both 'true' and 'real' in such sentences as 'The whale is a true mammal.' and 'That is a real duck.' have a comparable feature. Comparable, but not the same: 'That is a duck.' can be said of a decoy or a toy duck, but 'That is a real duck.' cannot, so these sentences are not truth-functional equivalents. Thus, the very rarity of the E-feature and related facts and their persistence throughout all form 106 sentences should lead one to suppose that 'right' is univocal over all such sentences. If one supposes otherwise, then one is faced with the task of constructing a variety of senses each one of which must possess these features. At a minimum, it seems evident that the different senses cannot be very different.

186

'Right' and 'Wrong'

Not only is it hard to envisage *how* 'right' could be ambiguous, it is also most unclear how one could *show* it to be ambiguous over form 106 sentences. Take any such sentence:

(125)   That is the right thing for you to do.

We can hold in abeyance the question of whether or not 125 is ambiguous, for what is important is that any ambiguity possessed by 125 will be possessed by its counterpart:

(125a)   That is the thing for you to do.

Now, since 'right' does not appear at all in 125a, it is something of a mystery how it could play a role in whatever ambiguities 125a may possess. And, a fortiori, it is implausible to suppose that it plays a role in any ambiguities possessed by 125. Since this argument applies to any form 106 sentence, I don't see how 'right' could be shown to be ambiguous in or over any such sentences.

An ambiguist might claim that 'right' is univocal over form 106 sentences only because the syntactical situation does not allow its other senses to be realized. But now, take any two sentences over which, according to your immediate linguistic intuitions, 'right' (or 'wrong') is ambiguous. Many people might say that 'right' is ambiguous over the following sentences:

(126)   What he said is right.
(127)   What he did was morally right.

Yet I suspect that according to most people's intuition of synonymy, 'right' is univocal over 126 and 115 ('Samuel Gompers' is the right answer to question 37.') and over 127 and 120 ('That is the morally right thing for you to do.') But if, by the foregoing argument, 'right' is univocal over 115 and 120, then this might lead you to give up the idea that it is ambiguous over 126 and 127. It might lead you, but it does not force you to give up the idea. Still, the fact that any use of 'right' in a non-form 106 sentence can be matched by our intuitions to a use of 'right' in a form 106 sentence and the fact that 'right' is univocal over all the latter uses together constitute persuasive grounds for saying that 'right' and 'wrong' are univocal over all their uses.

However persuasive this last argument may be, it is really rather flimsy. The univocity of 'right' within form 106 seems well supported, but the univocity of 'right' overall is not. So far the sole support for the latter is immediate linguistic intuition—an untrustworthy guide, especially when isolating the contributions of one word in two disparate constructions. We must be able to say what, syntactically, 'right' is doing in some environment if we are to describe 'right' 's semantic properties there and relate them to those in another environment.

The point here is crucial. The literature on the semantics of 'right' has gone wrong just because of its naïveté regarding the syntax of 'right'. Little thought has been given to the matter at all, it being assumed that, in some fairly straightforward way, 'right' is predicated of actions and other sorts of things. Of course, 'right' is supposed to be a "value predicate" like 'good' and 'punk', and controversy has raged over whether and how value predicates differ from factual predicates, but even that has been treated as a semantic issue. What goes unnoticed is that the grammar of 'right' and 'wrong' is unmatched by any other English word; they operate in a unique array of syntactical structures and, as we have already observed, in unique ways within some of those structures.

Unfortunately, grammarians have yet to settle upon a happy

analysis of these structures and their interrelations. In consequence, a validation of an account of the semantics of 'right' must wait upon advances in syntactical research. This might be used as a decent excuse for quitting here. After all, the philosophical points seem plain enough already. Whatever else may be true about 'right', it seems sufficiently clear that 'right' is univocal over form 106 sentences, and that a moral judgment of that form is justified in exactly the same way as any other judgment of that form, namely by justifying the correlative form 106a judgment. Thus, whatever else may be true about 'right', the news is unlikely to contain any more information about morality than the preceding has.

Nonetheless, I fancy the heroic course of offering some speculations bolstered by an assortment of palpable facts and plausible, though unproven, hypotheses. Even with the speculations my account is incomplete, and even without them my polemical purposes are served. But the speculations help organize and explain some of the indisputable facts, and therefore seem deserving of a hearing. Moreover, evidence of the utility of the hypotheses may prove of some aid to syntactical research.

What needs to be understood is what 'right' is predicated of in form 106 sentences. At first glance, 'right' here appears to be a syncategorematic adjective like 'good' and 'wee' and unlike 'bulbous' and 'wicked'. But that analysis suffers from at least two defects. First, intuition provides some reason to think that the 'right' in some form 106 sentences is the same 'right' in some non–form 106 sentences, but there is no reason, intuitive or otherwise, to think that 'right' is syncategorematic outside form 106. Secondly, that analysis fails to take cognizance of the E-feature. If 'right' modified any component of a form 106 sentence, then, so it seems, the form 106a sentence could not have the same associable truth-conditions, unless 'right' were some sort of semantically vacuous term—hardly a plausible option. This point would apply equally well even if 'right' could be predicated only in tandem with another term.

A well-marked exit from this dilemma is provided by the parallel between the E-feature of 'right' and a notorious fact about 'true': 'p' is true if and only if p. That is, the following are all truth-functionally equivalent.

(125)   That is the right thing for you to do.
(128)   It is true that that is the right thing for you to do.
(125a) That is the thing for you to do.
(128a) It is true that that is the thing for you to do.

And we may add on another.

(129)   It is right that that is the thing for you to do.

It seems clear that in 129 and in many other non–form 106 sentences 'right' is predicated of a proposition just as 'true' is in 128 and 128a. (Grammarians would say that 'right' and 'true' are predicated of sentences here, but it seems that propositions rather than sentences have a truth-value and, to coin a term, a righth-value.) By supposing that 'right' *always* works something like 'true' we can account for the E-feature; we simply take 'right' in 125 to be covertly predicated of the proposition expressed by sentence 125a, just as in 129 'right' is overtly predicated of that same proposition. (In the vernacular of transformational grammarians this means that in the deep structure of 125 'right' is predicated of sentence 125a.) Note that I have said that 128a and 129 are equivalent; they are also mutual paraphrases, but they are not synonymous. Later I shall attempt to distinguish 'right' from 'true', but for now I am concerned to show that 'right' always means (something like) 'true'.

'Right' and 'Wrong'

Working from this hypothesis, the task becomes one of showing that 'right' operates in the same way when not immediately succeeded by a noun phrase (i.e., outside form 106). The basic sentence form here is:

(130) NP_1 *copula* right.

Here it might seem that 'right' is used attributively, that it is predicated directly of actions and other sorts of things. But let us look more closely.

Among the most common constructions used as the NP_1 are 'for NP_1 to VP' and 'that NP_1 *inf* VP'. The two are virtually synonymous here.

(131)   For him to be the owner is right.
(132)   That he be the owner is right.

The sense of such sentences is unaltered by a transposition of these constructions and the use of 'it' as the ostensible subject.

(133)   It is right for him to be the owner.
(134)   It is right that he be the owner.

Ellipses of the 'for NP_1 to VP' are common here.

(135)   It was wrong to invite her.
(136)   To invite her was wrong.

A gerundival phrase serves the same purpose.

(137)   His being the owner is right.
(138)   Inviting her was wrong.

It would hardly be original for me to claim that such sentence components as 'for NP to VP' are really whole sentences embedded in a sentence just as 125a is a sentence embedded in 128a and 129; some grammarians have contended that a proper transformational analysis reveals just that. (The subject and predicate of such a sentence are obvious.) However, the issue is controversial and I shall not recite the arguments. Instead I shall simply accept the claim because it is plausible and makes sense of various facts regarding 'right'. The point then would be that in sentences like 131–138 'right' is predicated of the proposition expressed by the embedded sentence. This raises the problem of specifying the expressed proposition. A possible solution has been readied for us by the account of the modals; we need only treat the 'for NP to VP' and 'that NP *inf* VP' constructions here as sentences with indicators that the relevant System is an SI. (In that respect, these sentences are akin to imperative sentences.) Thus, reverting to the earlier symbolism, a sentence of the form 'It is right for n to v' is equivalent to 'It is true that (ideally) n v', and thus to '(ideally) n v'. The result here seems to jibe with intuition. An advantage of this reading is a suggested explanation of the choice of qualifying component in form 106 sentences: whenever 'for NP_3 to VP' is used, the relevant System is an SI, but when a prepositional or adverbial phrase follows 'time', 'answer', and the like, the relevant System may be an SA or an SI (e.g., depending on the question).*

---

* Some observations on the "moral sense" of 'right': Notice that sentences like 131–138 are most naturally used in moral and quasi-moral contexts. And, although philosophers are wont to speak of 'right acts' and 'right actions', in ordinary conversation such talk sounds rather quaint; when we discuss a moral matter with a form 106 sentence we talk about the *thing* for NP_3 to VP (e.g., for him to do), not the right act to perform. In some contexts 'thing' seems to be used only because of its extreme generality, but, I suggest, in moral contexts 'thing' is a dummy noun: it takes up a syntactic space without having semantic weight. So, the 'for-to' component does all the work there just as in sentences like 131 and 133. (Actually, the VP is often a dummy verb, 'do' or 'be', which refers back to the NP_1.) The reason that these constructions are used in and suggest a moral context has nothing to do

'Right' and 'Wrong'

Some other sentence structures remain to be studied. Look now at form 130 sentences which are like 134 (and thus like 131–138) except that the verb is not infinitival so that the component following 'that' could stand alone as a grammatically complete sentence 'S' (i.e., 'NP VP', 'n v').

(139)   It is right that he is the owner.
(140)   It is right that S
(129)   It is right that that is the thing for you to do.

Any form 140 sentence is equivalent to:

(140a)   It is true that S

Note carefully that 'S' may express a proposition in either an SA or an SI. Thus, 139 is unlike 134 in which 'true' is substitutable for 'right' only after the transformation has been effected. 'True' operates only on sentences that have the surface grammar of a sentence; 'right' operates on sentences whether or not they have the surface grammar of a sentence.

A further difference between 139 and 134, and between 129 and 128a, is that form 140 sentences are syntactically ambiguous. In their alternative interpretation they, unlike 134, imply 'S', and, like 134, 'It is true that (ideally) S'. The 'S' of the first implication may express a proposition in either an SA or an SI, but the 'S' of the second implication is marked to express a proposition in an SI. The first implication is akin to the relation

---

with the meaning of 'right' per se. Rather, to put the matter crudely, the assessment of an action or state in and of itself, not qua this or that (e.g., a move in a game, a means to an end), is peculiar to moral judgments. The embedded sentences of 131–138 present an action or state for assessment in an unqualified form, and therefore they are most naturally used for moral judgments. Form 106 sentences can do the same by naming the action or state in the first noun phrase and then using 'thing for NP₃ to do'.

between 'God forgives.' and 'God exists.'; if the implicans is false, the implicandum has a problematic truth-value. To mark this relation I shall bracket this 'S' and write the second interpretation as:

(140b)   [S] · It is true that (ideally) S

'Right' is not predicated of '[S]'; if it were, then 'wrong' in the same position would too. Compare:

(141)   It is wrong that she is the owner.
(141a)   It is false that S
(141b)   [S] · It is false that (ideally) S
(141c)   It is false that ([S] · (ideally) S)

Clearly, 141c is an erroneous reading.

I said that the ambiguity is syntactical. 'Right' is not ambiguous; it simply allows the ambiguity to be realized. (The fact that 'right' and 'wrong' are about the only words that allow the ambiguity to be realized is no evidence that the ambiguity is morphological; it is obvious already that 'right' and 'wrong' are syntactically special.) In both interpretations 'right' is predicated of a proposition, a different one in each case. Given the hypothesis that 'right' means something like 'true', 140a requires no explanation, but 140b does. Some insight is gained by studying another sentence structure.

Take the following sentence:

(142)   Something is wrong.

This has three interpretations, in only two of which can it be read as '($\exists$x) Wx'. If 'x' ranges over all propositions, 142 is like 141a; here 142 would be true if 'What he said is wrong.' is true. If 'x' can range over only propositions expressed by sentences marked as expressing propositions in an SI, 142 is like

131–138; here 142 would be true if 'For her to be the owner is wrong.' is true. In its third interpretation 142 is like 141b except that the existence claim is explicit; here 142 is true if and only if 'S · It is false that (ideally) S' is true. The difference between the first two and the third interpretations is syntactically well marked. In the former, 142 is paraphrasable as 'There exists an x such that x is wrong.'. Not so the latter; it must be paraphrased as 'There exists something x and x is something that is wrong.'. I shall explain this.

The third interpretation is actually the most common use of 142. Some examples:

(143)   Something is wrong with the car; it stalls at high speeds.—It's got a clogged fuel line. That's what's wrong.

(144)   Something is wrong with Vincent; he's been depressed all day.—Not surprising; he's been fired.

(145)   Something is wrong with that proof. Aha! Step 3 is illegitimate.

(146)   Something is wrong with his assertion.—You bet there is. It's false; that's what's wrong with it.

(147)   Something is wrong with American foreign policy, morally wrong, for it presumes to dictate the conditions under which every nation shall live.

When completely spelled out in a single sentence, such sentences have the form:

(148)   The thing that *copula* wrong with n *copula* that n v
(143a) The thing that is wrong with the car is that it (the car) has a clogged fuel line.

Such sentences are alterable in various ways. The 'thing that' is replaceable by 'what'. The 'with n' is deletable if the n is understood or unknown. Or 'with n' may sometimes be replaced by 'about n', 'in n', 'here', or similar prepositional or adverbial phrases. The 'that n v' (e.g., 'that it has a clogged fuel line') has various elliptical forms (e.g., 'it's having a clogged fuel line', 'a clogged fuel line', 'the fuel line'), and may be transposed to the beginning of the sentence (e.g., 'A clogged fuel line is the thing that is wrong with the car.').

But the important point here is the alterations that cannot be made, namely those in the initial noun phrase. The NP_1 of this sort of form 130 sentence must be 'what(ever)' or a 'thing' phrase (e.g., 'anything', 'two things') or 'that' (or 'which') preceded by a 'thing' phrase. Another possibility is to transpose the 'that n v' in front of a 'that'; then the sentence preceding 'that' is composed of some ellipsis of 'that n v' used as either a predicate nominative with 'it' as its subject or as the subject with a 'thing' phrase as its predicate nominative. A variant of this puts 'that n v' or some ellipsis of it in front of the initial copula; then a 'thing' phrase and 'wrong' follow the copula. In brief, we can say here 'A clogged fuel line is the thing that is wrong with the car.' or 'A clogged fuel line is something wrong with the car.', but we cannot say 'A clogged fuel line is wrong with the car.'.

It should now be obvious that in its third interpretation 142 is composed of one sentence, 'that n v', that is operated upon twice, just as it is in a form 148 sentence. It is said that 'Something is that n v' and 'Something (i.e., that n v) is wrong'. Note that in 148 (and thus 142) 'thing' refers not to 'n v' but to 'that n v' as is indicated by the fact that 'that n v' is replaceable by a gerundival phrase (e.g., 'it's having a clogged fuel line'). We noted in 131–138 that this syntactically marks the sentence as expressing a proposition in an SI. So, to say 'something is that n v (e.g., it's having a clogged fuel line)' is to say

'Right' and 'Wrong'

'n v', and to say 'that n v is wrong' is to say 'It is false that (ideally) n v'. This analysis explains the ambiguity of 140. In 140, 'right' is the predicate of 'it'; in 140a 'it' refers to 'S', but in 140b 'it' refers to 'that S'.

Even if all the foregoing is admitted, the univocity of 'right' is not yet vouchsafed. There remain other candidates for the NP_1 of form 130 sentences. Fortunately this lot is readily disposed of. Many of them employ the derivative sense; the remainder have equivalents in one of the types already discussed. In general, if the NP_1 refers to a thing (object, person), the sentence is equivalent to a form 106 sentence whose NP_2 is some genus term for the NP_1. Actually, we should speak here of utterances, not sentences because the NP_1 may be a pronoun and because the choice of NP_2 may be dictated by the speaker's intentions, what he has in mind as the respect in which the NP_1 is right. Similarly, if the NP_1 refers to an action or state, the sentence finds an equivalent among sentences like 131–138.

(149)   The time (now) is right for the attack.
(149a) Now is the right time for the attack (to begin).
(150)   Murder is wrong.
(150a) For someone to murder someone is wrong.
(150b) It is wrong (for someone) to murder (someone).

Since such form 130 sentences are equivalent to a sentence in which 'right' is predicated of a proposition, they can be treated accordingly. I say 'can', not 'must', because the sole reason I have for so treating them is that it seems permissible and required for a simple, unified, comprehensive account of 'right'—not an insubstantial motive at that.

A pleasant upshot of my account of 'right' is that it explains our intuition that 'morally right' bears a close relation to 'morally ought'. If 'n ought to v' expresses a moral law (e.g., 'n' is 'everyone'), then it is equivalent to 'For n to v is right'. The former is equivalent to '(ideally) (x) (Fx ⊃ Vx)' (e.g., 'F' is 'a person'), and so is the latter. However, if 'n ought to v' expresses a particular moral judgment, then it implies '(ideally) n v or —C', but 'For n to v is right' implies simply '(ideally) n v', and thus is closer to 'n must v'. If this jibes with intuition then my two accounts confirm each other. Unfortunately, going by the philosophical literature, our intuitions on the details of this matter are hazy.

I would guess that there are some who might bridle a bit at the idea that 'right' and 'wrong' are not value predicates comparable to 'nice' and 'naughty' but rather univocal semantic predicates fully comparable to 'true' and 'false'. Yet, all sorts of circumstantial evidence supports the idea. Look at the etymology of 'right' and 'true': they developed quite independently, yet both words trace back to words meaning 'straight'. Further, each of them has developed a network of immediately and naturally related senses, and the two networks overlap, intersect, or are tangential at point after point (especially if their adverbial and verbal forms are included). For example, both words have uses in which they are paraphrasable by 'straight', 'proper', 'real', and 'very'—and each of these paraphrases actually represents a cluster of uses (and the clusters overlap each other). And if a "moral overtone" is wanted, 'true' has a use with it: 'a true friend'. In addition, in the sense we are concerned with, both words have comparative and superlative forms having quite limited use. Also, both words are modifiable by roughly the same class of adverbs, a quite select set (e.g., 'not', 'quite', 'so', 'absolutely', 'completely', 'perfectly'). And finally there is the fact that in some environments 'right' is obviously roughly synonymous with 'true'; my whole argument has been that in the other environments what is not so obvious is the syntactical structure.

Still, quite independently of any hard facts to the contrary, some resistance will be made to the claim that 'right' is very like 'true'. No doubt the main resistance is merely an expression of a complete reliance on immediate linguistic intuition, but I would suppose that some resistance is traceable as much to misconceptions about 'true' as to misconceptions about 'right'. We rivet our attention on the fact that 'p' is equivalent to ' 'p' is true'; we take this to be a unique fact, sufficient to define 'true'. So we think that truth is some sort of simple, absolute property or relation existing for all times and all places without admitting of division, changes, or degrees. We forget that something can be true *of* one thing but not another, or true *in* some place or *at* some time but not another; we forget that something can come to be true or cease to be true or be partly true or (not) very true or (not) so true or (not) completely or perfectly true. Perhaps the fact that 'right' also possesses the feature of being true-functionally eliminable will help us realize that that feature is inadequate to define either 'true' or 'right'.

And now the crucial point is that 'right' and 'true' are not synonymous. Though both are metalinguistic predicates, syntactically they are still very different. Even when they are mutual paraphrases in some environment they still differ. Though we may say 'That is true.' or 'That is right.', we do not speak of 'right statements' any more than of 'true answers'. Nor are these adjectives qualifiable by exactly the same adverbs; what someone says may be exactly or precisely right, but not exactly or precisely true. Actually 'true' and 'right' are never really intersubstitutable; though we may say 'Is that right?' or 'Is that true?' in response to an utterance, these sentences are not used on the same occasions or uttered with the same intonation contours.

However, the semantic differences between 'true' and 'right' are subtle and difficult to specify. Part of the semantic difference seems connected to the syntactic difference that only 'right' operates upon sentences marked to express propositions in an SI. Thus, 'true' seems to be more closely tied to the notion of factuality. A related difference is caught by Ziff's claim that " 'false' invokes a factor of deceit." [1] In defense of this he cites various naturally related uses of 'false': 'a false face', 'a false front', 'a false friend'. He does not mention the salient fact that 'false' derives from a word meaning 'to deceive'. Nor does he seem to recognize that 'true' appears to involve a denial of a factor of deceit. Note that 'true' is often the antonym of 'false' in these other uses: 'a true friend'. So, my suggestion is that the meaning of 'true' might be expressed as 'faithful to the facts'. (Cf.: 'a true copy'.) 'Right' and 'wrong' seem free of this connection with deceit. 'Wrong' derives from a word meaning 'awry', 'crooked', which is simply the opposite of 'right' 's original meaning of 'straight'. Thus, they seem to be more general terms, free of the restrictions on 'true' and 'false'.

This hypothesis seems borne out by the kinds of illocutions of which 'true' and 'false' are normally predicated. In contrast with other declarative illocutions (e.g., comments), statements and assertions seem especially likely to be made where a question of deceit might arise. So too, we generally use 'true' and 'false' (e.g., 'That's (not) true'), not 'right' or 'wrong' when we admit, confess, or deny some charge, allegation, or other incriminating remark. On the other hand, 'right' and 'wrong' (e.g., 'That's (not) right'), not 'true' and 'false' are used when we do mathematics (e.g., check over a computation), since there no question of deceit normally arises.

Perhaps the word 'true' should be of interest to epistemologists and metaphysicians. I rather doubt it, but in any case 'true' is probably important to metalinguists. And if my account of 'right' is right, then 'right' should have the same interest and importance; indeed it should have even more since it seems to be a more general term than 'true'. But that is of little interest to me. For myself, ethics studies what is most important—it is the study of whatever is most important—and thus ethics is the most important study. A moral philosopher should be interested in what is morally right, but he will learn no more about it by studying the word 'right' than he would by studying the word 'true': nothing. Unless this last claim is wrong, a serious moral philosopher is wasting his time worrying about the meaning of 'right' (i.e., about the truth of any of my previous claims).

Notes

Chapter One

1. Bentham, p. 4.
2. Prichard, pp. 90–92.
3. Ross, p. 2.
4. See Ross, p. 3; Sidgwick, p. 29; Ewing (1), p. 123.
5. Ewing (1), chap. 4.
6. Ewing (2), p. 129.
7. Prichard, p. 91.
8. Sidgwick, p. 34.
9. Ewing (2), p. 132.
10. Prichard, pp. 90–91.
11. Moore, p. 12.
12. Ewing (2), p. 132.
13. Moore, p. 40.
14. Ayer, pp. 102–113.
15. Hare (1), pp. 60–62.
16. Casteñeda, pp. 225–226.

17. Gauthier, p. 12.
18. Hare (1), p. 28.
19. Hare (1), pp. 163–179.
20. Hare (1), pp. 4–5.
21. Hare (1), p. 29.
22. See Hare (1), p. 1; Nowell-Smith, p. 11.
23. Hare (1), pp. 168–169.
24. Nowell-Smith, pp. 267–268.
25. See Austin (2), p. 159; Gauthier, p. 15.
26. Austin (3), pp. 66–71.

Chapter Two

1. Ziff (1), p. 153.
2. Katz and Martin, p. 488.
3. Quine (2), p. 131.
4. Wittgenstein (1), p. 58.
5. Wittgenstein (1), p. 30.
6. Ziff (2), p. 44.
7. Ziff (1), pp. 144–145.
8. Fodor and Freed (1).
9. See Ziff (2), p. 190.
10. Quine (2), p. 103.
11. Sommers, pp. 265–266.
12. Alston, pp. 36–39.
13. Fodor and Freed (1), p. 8.
14. Searle (1).
15. Ziff (1), p. 144.
16. Austin (1), pp. 92–93.
17. See Fodor and Freed (2).
18. See Mannison.
19. Austin (1), p. 115.
20. Urmson.
21. See Searle (2); Geach (1) and (2).
22. Hare (2), p. 14.

Notes

Chapter Three

1. Ziff (2), pp. 191–193.
2. See Hart and Honoré, pp. 31–38.
3. Ehrman, Appendix.
4. Wittgenstein (3), p. 37.
5. Anscombe (2).
6. Margolis, p. 48.
7. Margolis, p. 46.

Chapter Four

1. Lévi-Strauss, p. 88.
2. Piaget (3), p. 340.
3. Piaget (3), p. 352.
4. Nietzsche, p. 197.
5. See Piaget (1), pp. 237–240.
6. Hume, pp. 469–470.
7. See Hare (1), pp. 68–69.
8. Goodman, pp. 63–64.
9. Rawls (1) and (2).
10. Wittgenstein (5), p. 147.
11. See Kuhn; Putnam.
12. Quine (2), p. 59.
13. Piaget (2), p. 7.
14. Piaget (3), pp. 139–147.

Chapter Five

1. Ziff (2), p. 117.

Bibliography

Alston, William P. *Philosophy of Language*. Englewood Cliffs, N.J.: Prentice-Hall, 1964.

Anscombe, Gertrude E. M. (1) "Brute Facts," in *Analysis*, 18 (1958), 69–72.

———. (2) "Modern Moral Philosophy," in *Philosophy*, 33 (1958), 1–19.

Austin, John Langshaw. (1) *How to Do Things with Words*. New York: Oxford University Press, 1965.

———. (2) "Ifs and Cans," in Austin, *Philosophical Papers*. Oxford: Clarendon Press, 1961.

———. (3) "Other Minds," in Austin, *Philosophical Papers*. Oxford: Clarendon Press, 1961.

Ayer, Alfred Jules. *Language, Truth, and Logic*. London: V. Gollancz, 1946.

Bentham, Jeremy. *An Introduction to the Principles of Morals and Legislation*. New York: Hafner, 1948.

Casteñeda, Hector-Neri. "Imperatives, Decisions, and "Oughts"," in Casteñeda and George Nakhnikian, eds., *Morality and the*

Bibliography

Language of Conduct (Detroit: Wayne State University Press, 1965).

Ehrman, Madeline. *The Meanings of the Modals in Present-Day American English*. The Hague: Mouton, 1966.

Ewing, Alfred Cyril. (1) *The Definition of Good*. New York: Macmillan, 1947.

———. (2) "Subjectivism and Naturalism in Ethics," in *Mind*, 210 (1944), 120–141.

Fodor, J. A. and R. B. Freed. (1) "Pains, Puns, Persons, and Pronouns," in *Analysis*, 22 (1961), 6–9.

———. (2) "Some Types of Ambiguous Tokens," in *Analysis*, 24 (1963), 19–23.

Gauthier, David P. *Practical Reasoning*. Oxford: Clarendon Press, 1963.

Geach, Peter. (1) "Ascriptivism," in *Philosophical Review*, 69 (1960), 423–432.

———. (2) "Assertions," in *Philosophical Review*, 74 (1965), 449–465.

Goodman, Nelson. *Fact, Fiction, and Forecast*. New York: Bobbs-Merrill, 1965.

Grice, H. Paul. "Causal Theory of Perception," in *Proceedings of the Aristotelian Society*, Suppl. vol. 25 (1961), pp. 121–152.

Hare, Richard M. (1) *The Language of Morals*. Oxford: Clarendon Press, 1952.

———. (2) "Meaning and Speech Acts," in *Philosophical Review*, 79 (1970), 3–24.

Hart, H. L. A. and A. M. Honoré, *Causation in the Law*. Oxford: Clarendon Press, 1959.

Hume, David. *A Treatise of Human Nature*. L. A. Selby-Bigge, ed. Oxford: Clarendon Press, 1888.

Jespersen, Otto. *A Modern English Grammar*. 7 vols. Heidelberg: Carl Winters Universitätsbuchhandlung, 1931.

Joos, Martin. *The English Verb*. Madison: University of Wisconsin Press, 1964.

Bibliography

Kant, Immanuel. (1) *Foundations of the Metaphysics of Morals,* in Lewis White Beck, ed. *Critique of Practical Reason.* Chicago: University of Chicago Press, 1950.

——. (2) "On a Supposed Right to Tell Lies from Benevolent Motives," in Thomas Kingsmill Abbott, ed., *Kant's Critique of Practical Reason* (London: Longmans, Green, 1909).

Katz, Jerold J. and Edward Martin, Jr. "The Synonymy of Actives and Passives," in *Philosophical Review,* 76 (1967), 476–491.

Kohlberg, Lawrence. (1) "The Development of Children's Orientations toward a Moral Order: 1. Sequence in the Development of Moral Thought," in *Vita Humana,* 6 (1963), 11–33.

——. (2) "Development of Moral Character and Ideology," in M. L. Hoffman, ed., *Review of Child Development Research.* Vol. I (New York: Russell Sage, 1964).

——. (3) "Moral Development and Identification," in H. Stevenson, ed., *Child Psychology, 62nd Yearbook Nat. Soc. Stud. Educ.* (Chicago: University of Chicago Press, 1963).

——. (4) "Moral Education in the Schools: A Developmental View," in *School Review,* 74 (1966), 1–30.

——. (5) "Moral and Religious Education and the Public Schools: A Developmental View," in Theodore Sizer, ed., *Religion and Public Education* (Boston: Houghton Mifflin, 1967).

——. (6) *Moral Development.* New York: Holt, Rinehart, and Winston, 1972.

Kuhn, Thomas S. *The Structure of Scientific Revolution.* Chicago: University of Chicago Press, 1961.

Lévi-Strauss, Claude. *The Elementary Structures of Kinship.* Boston: Beacon Press, 1969.

Mannison, Donald S. "On the Alleged Ambiguity of Strawson's P-Predicates," in *Analysis,* 23 (1962), 3–5.

Margolis, Joseph. "The Analysis of 'Ought'," in *Australasian Journal of Philosophy,* 48 (1970), 44–53.

Mayo, Bernard. (1) *Ethics and the Moral Life.* London: Macmillan, 1958.

Bibliography

———. (2) "On the Lehrer-Taylor Analysis of 'can'-Statements," in *Mind*, 67 (1968), 271–278.

Moore, George Edward. *Principia Ethica*. Cambridge: Cambridge University Press, 1962.

Nietzsche, Friedrich. *The Birth of Tragedy and The Geneaology of Morals*. Garden City, N.Y.: Doubleday, 1956.

Nowell-Smith, P. H. *Ethics*. Baltimore: Penguin Books, 1954.

Piaget, Jean. (1) *The Child's Conception of Causality*. Totowa, N.J.: Littlefield, Adams, 1965.

———. (2) *Judgment and Reasoning in the Child*. Paterson, N.J.: Littlefield, Adams, 1964.

———. (3) *The Moral Judgment of the Child*. New York: Collier Books, 1962.

Prichard, Harold A. *Moral Obligation*. Oxford: Clarendon Press, 1949.

Putnam, Hilary. "The Analytic and the Synthetic," in Herbert Feigel and Grover Maxwell, eds., *Minnesota Studies in the Philosophy of Science*, Vol. III (Minneapolis: University of Minnesota Press, 1962).

Quine, W. V. O. (1) "Two Dogmas of Empiricism," in Quine, *From a Logical Point of View* (New York: Harper & Row, 1963).

———. (2) *Word and Object*. New York: Technology Press, and John Wiley and Sons, 1960.

Rawls, John. (1) "Outline of a Decision Procedure for Ethics," in *Philosophical Review*, 60 (1951), 177–197.

———. (2) *A Theory of Justice*. Cambridge: Harvard University Press, 1972.

Richman, Robert. J. "Ambiguity and Intuition," in *Mind*, 68 (1959), 87–92.

Ross, Sir William David. *The Right and the Good*. Oxford: Clarendon Press, 1930.

Searle, John R. (1) "Austin on Locutionary and Illocutionary Acts," in *Philosophical Review*, 77 (1968), 405–424.

———. (2) "Meaning and Speech Acts," in *Philosophical Review*, 71 (1962), 423–432.

Bibliography

Sidgwick, Henry. *The Methods of Ethics*. Chicago: University of Chicago Press, 1962.

Sommers, Fred. "Predicability," in Max Black, ed., *Philosophy in America* (Ithaca: Cornell University Press, 1965).

Taylor, Paul W. *Normative Discourse*. Englewood Cliffs, N.J.: Prentice-Hall, 1961.

Twaddell, W. F. *The English Verb Auxiliaries*. Providence: Brown University Press, 1960.

Urmson, J. O. "Parenthetical Verbs," in *Mind*, 61 (1952), 13–38.

Wertheimer, Roger. "Conditions," in *Journal of Philosophy*, 65 (1968), 355–364.

White, Morton. "On What Could Have Happened," in *Philosophical Review*, 77 (1968), 73–89.

Whitely, C. H. "On Defining "Moral"," in *Analysis*, 20 (1960), 141–144.

Wittgenstein, Ludwig. (1) *The Blue and Brown Books*. Oxford: Basil Blackwell, 1964.

——. (2) "A Lecture on Ethics," in *Philosophical Review*, 74 (1965), 3–12.

——. (3) *Philosophical Investigations*. New York: Macmillan, 1960.

——. (4) *Remarks on the Foundations of Mathematics*. Oxford: Basil Blackwell, 1964.

——. (5) *Tractatus Logico-Philosophicus*. London: Routledge and Kegan Paul, 1961.

Ziff, Paul. (1) *Philosophic Turnings*. Ithaca: Cornell University Press, 1966.

——. (2) *Semantic Analysis*. Ithaca: Cornell University Press, 1960.

Index

Index

Definition, 40, 47, 84, 103n, 178-179
see also Account
Derivative sense of 'right', 181-182, 197
Developmentalist theory, *see* Kohlberg, L., *and* Piaget, J.
Dewey, J., 146n
Doctrine of Moral Senses, 6-17, 19-20, 22, 26, 32n, 45
Doctrine of Practical Senses, 20-32, 45

E(eliminability)-feature, 185-187, 190, 199
Ehrman, M., 79n, 117
Etymology, 58-60, 78, 130-132, 134, 198, 200
Ewing, A. C., 8, 14n, 15n
Extensional considerations, 36, 60-61, 102n

Facts, 85, 103, 114-115, 122, 125n, 131, 149, 158-160, 173-174
'False', 200
see also 'True'
FF sentences, 28-32, 43, 70-75
Fodor, J. A., 54, 68
'For-to' component, 183-185, 191-192
Freed, R. B., 54, 68

Gauthier, D. P., 20
'Good', 3-4, 6, 8, 18n, 62n, 76n, 132, 134, 151-152, 188-189
Goodman, N., 85, 165, 166n, 169-171
Grice, H. P., 30, 129
see also Conversation

Hare, R. M., 17n, 18n, 22-23, 28, 35, 76n
Hume, D., 2, 150-151, 156-159, 165

Illocutions, 18-28, 46, 47, 50, 141, 162-164, 200
multiple potential of, 28-32, 67-76, 119-121, 139-140
see also Propositions
Imperatives, 19, 22-24, 118-119, 139-140, 145n, 162-163, 172n, 192
Implicatures, *see* Conversation
Intuition (linguistic), 8-9, 32n, 35-38, 41-42, 47, 65, 178-179, 187-188, 192, 197-198
Intuitionism, 2-17, 20n, 27n, 160

Jespersen, O., 79n
Job, 144-145

Kant, I., 13-14, 26, 90, 117, 118, 147, 173n
Katz, J., 35
Kirilov, 106, 145, 173-174
Kohlberg, L., 142, 147, 148
Kuhn, T., 5n

Language, 41-42, 161-165
Law, 72, 85, 88-92, 100-102, 115-117, 119-121, 128, 136, 141, 160-173
Lévi-Strauss, C., 142n
Linguistics, 16, 35, 38-39, 43-45, 138, 162-164, 175-177, 179
Logic, 95n, 101, 121-123, 134, 138-139, 161, 165-172

Margolis, J., 132-134
Martin, E., 35
Mathematics, 121-123, 138, 143, 166-172, 200-201
'May', 64n, 80-84, 98n, 125-126, 167n
Mayo, B., 18n, 85n
M-criterion, 7-10, 18n
Meta-ethics, 1-5, 33, 43n, 49, 99, 146n, 151-152, 156

Index